THE PELICAN SHAKESPEARE
GENERAL EDITORS

STEPHEN ORGEL
A. R. BRAUNMULLER

The Tragedy of Othello the Moor of Venice

Edmund Kean (1787-1833) as a diabolical Othello,
one of his greatest roles. He also played a superlatively
villainous Iago, and his final performance in 1833 was as
Othello to the Iago of his equally famous son Charles.
(Engraving after a drawing by J. W. Gear.)

William Shakespeare

The Tragedy of Othello
the Moor of Venice

EDITED BY RUSS McDONALD

PENGUIN BOOKS

PENGUIN BOOKS
Published by the Penguin Group
Penguin Group (USA) Inc., 375 Hudson Street, New York, New York 10014, U.S.A.
Penguin Group (Canada), 90 Eglinton Avenue East, Suite 700, Toronto, Ontario,
Canada M4P 2Y3 (a division of Pearson Penguin Canada Inc.)
Penguin Books Ltd, 80 Strand, London WC2R 0RL, England
Penguin Ireland, 25 St Stephen's Green, Dublin 2, Ireland (a division of Penguin Books Ltd)
Penguin Group (Australia), 250 Camberwell Road, Camberwell, Victoria 3124,
Australia (a division of Pearson Australia Group Pty Ltd)
Penguin Books India Pvt Ltd, 11 Community Centre, Panchsheel Park,
New Delhi – 110 017, India
Penguin Group (NZ), 67 Apollo Drive, Rosedale, North Shore 0632, New Zealand
(a division of Pearson New Zealand Ltd)
Penguin Books (South Africa) (Pty) Ltd, 24 Sturdee Avenue, Rosebank,
Johannesburg 2196, South Africa

Penguin Books Ltd, Registered Offices: 80 Strand, London WC2R 0RL, England

The Tragedy of Othello the Moor of Venice edited
by Gerald Eades Bentley published in the
United States of America in Penguin Books 1958
Revised edition published 1970
This new edition edited by Russ McDonald published 2001

30 29 28 27

Copyright © Penguin Books Inc., 1958, 1970
Copyright © Penguin Putnam Inc., 2001
All rights reserved

ISBN 978-0-14-071463-0
(CIP data available)

Printed in the United States of America
Set in Adobe Garamond
Designed by Virginia Norey

Contents

Publisher's Note

IT IS ALMOST half a century since the first volumes of the Pelican Shakespeare appeared under the general editorship of Alfred Harbage. The fact that a new edition, rather than simply a revision, has been undertaken reflects the profound changes textual and critical studies of Shakespeare have undergone in the past twenty years. For the new Pelican series, the texts of the plays and poems have been thoroughly revised in accordance with recent scholarship, and in some cases have been entirely reedited. New introductions and notes have been provided in all the volumes. But the new Shakespeare is also designed as a successor to the original series; the previous editions have been taken into account, and the advice of the previous editors has been solicited where it was feasible to do so.

Certain textual features of the new Pelican Shakespeare should be particularly noted. All lines are numbered that contain a word, phrase, or allusion explained in the glossarial notes. In addition, for convenience, every tenth line is also numbered, in italics when no annotation is indicated. The intrusive and often inaccurate place headings inserted by early editors are omitted (as is becoming standard practice), but for the convenience of those who miss them, an indication of locale now appears as the first item in the annotation of each scene.

In the interest of both elegance and utility, each speech prefix is set in a separate line when the speaker's lines are in verse, except when those words form the second half of a verse line. Thus the verse form of the speech is kept visually intact. What is printed as verse and what is printed as prose has, in general, the authority of the original texts. Departures from the original texts in this regard have only the authority of editorial tradition and the judgment of the Pelican editors; and, in a few instances, are admittedly arbitrary.

The Theatrical World

ECONOMIC REALITIES determined the theatrical world in which Shakespeare's plays were written, performed, and received. For centuries in England, the primary theatrical tradition was nonprofessional. Craft guilds (or "mysteries") provided religious drama – mystery plays – as part of the celebration of religious and civic festivals, and schools and universities staged classical and neoclassical drama in both Latin and English as part of their curricula. In these forms, drama was established and socially acceptable. Professional theater, in contrast, existed on the margins of society. The acting companies were itinerant; playhouses could be any available space – the great halls of the aristocracy, town squares, civic halls, inn yards, fair booths, or open fields – and income was sporadic, dependent on the passing of the hat or on the bounty of local patrons. The actors, moreover, were considered little better than vagabonds, constantly in danger of arrest or expulsion.

In the late 1560s and 1570s, however, English professional theater began to gain respectability. Wealthy aristocrats fond of drama – the Lord Admiral, for example, or the Lord Chamberlain – took acting companies under their protection so that the players technically became members of their households and were no longer subject to arrest as homeless or masterless men. Permanent theaters were first built at this time as well, allowing the companies to control and charge for entry to their performances.

Shakespeare's livelihood, and the stunning artistic explosion in which he participated, depended on pragmatic and architectural effort. Professional theater requires ways to restrict access to its offerings; if it does not, and admission fees cannot be charged, the actors do not get paid, the costumes go to a pawnbroker, and there is no such thing as a professional, ongoing theatrical tradition. The answer to that economic need arrived in the late 1560s and 1570s with the creation of the so-called public or amphitheater playhouse. Recent discoveries indicate that the precursor of the Globe playhouse in London (where Shakespeare's mature plays were presented) and the Rose theater (which presented Christopher Marlowe's plays and some of Shakespeare's earliest ones) was the Red Lion theater of 1567. Archaeological studies of the foundations of the Rose and Globe theaters have revealed that the open-air theater of the 1590s and later was probably a polygonal building with fourteen to twenty or twenty-four sides, multistoried, from 75 to 100 feet in diameter, with a raised, partly covered "thrust" stage that projected into a group of standing patrons, or "groundlings," and a covered gallery, seating up to 2,500 or more (very crowded) spectators.

These theaters might have been about half full on any given day, though the audiences were larger on holidays or when a play was advertised, as old and new were, through printed playbills posted around London. The metropolitan area's late-Tudor, early-Stuart population (circa 1590–1620) has been estimated at about 150,000 to 250,000. It has been supposed that in the mid-1590s there were about 15,000 spectators per week at the public theaters; thus, as many as 10 percent of the local population went to the theater regularly. Consequently, the theaters' repertories – the plays available for this experienced and frequent audience – had to change often: in the month between September 15 and October 15, 1595, for instance, the Lord Admiral's Men performed twenty-eight times in eighteen different plays.

Since natural light illuminated the amphitheaters' stages, performances began between noon and two o'clock and ran without a break for two or three hours. They often concluded with a jig, a fencing display, or some other nondramatic exhibition. Weather conditions determined the season for the amphitheaters: plays were performed every day (including Sundays, sometimes, to clerical dismay) except during Lent – the forty days before Easter – or periods of plague, or sometimes during the summer months when law courts were not in session and the most affluent members of the audience were not in London.

To a modern theatergoer, an amphitheater stage like that of the Rose or Globe would appear an unfamiliar mixture of plainness and elaborate decoration. Much of the structure was carved or painted, sometimes to imitate marble; elsewhere, as under the canopy projecting over the stage, to represent the stars and the zodiac. Appropriate painted canvas pictures (of Jerusalem, for example, if the play was set in that city) were apparently hung on the wall behind the acting area, and tragedies were accompanied by black hangings, presumably something like crepe festoons or bunting. Although these theaters did not employ what we would call scenery, early modern spectators saw numerous large props, such as the "bar" at which a prisoner stood during a trial, the "mossy bank" where lovers reclined, an arbor for amorous conversation, a chariot, gallows, tables, trees, beds, thrones, writing desks, and so forth. Audiences might learn a scene's location from a sign (reading "Athens," for example) carried across the stage (as in Bertolt Brecht's twentieth-century productions). Equally captivating (and equally irritating to the theater's enemies) were the rich costumes and personal props the actors used: the most valuable items in the surviving theatrical inventories are the swords, gowns, robes, crowns, and other items worn or carried by the performers.

Magic appealed to Shakespeare's audiences as much as it does to us today, and the theater exploited many deceptive and spectacular devices. A winch in the loft above the stage, called "the heavens," could lower and raise actors playing gods, goddesses, and other supernatural figures to and from the main acting area, just as one or more trapdoors permitted entrances and exits to and from the area, called "hell," beneath the stage. Actors wore elementary makeup such as wigs, false beards, and face paint, and they employed pig's bladders filled with animal blood to make wounds seem more real. They had rudimentary but effective ways of pretending to behead or hang a person. Supernumeraries (stagehands or actors not needed in a particular scene) could make thunder sounds (by shaking a metal sheet or rolling an iron ball down a chute) and show lightning (by blowing inflammable resin through tubes into a flame). Elaborate fireworks enhanced the effects of dragons flying through the air or imitated such celestial phenomena as comets, shooting stars, and multiple suns. Horses' hoofbeats, bells (located perhaps in the tower above the stage), trumpets and drums, clocks, cannon shots and gunshots, and the like were common sound effects. And the music of viols, cornets, oboes, and recorders was a regular feature of theatrical performances.

For two relatively brief spans, from the late 1570s to 1590 and from 1599 to 1614, the amphitheaters competed with the so-called private, or indoor, theaters, which originated as, or later represented themselves as, educational institutions training boys as singers for church services and court performances. These indoor theaters had two features that were distinct from the amphitheaters': their personnel and their playing spaces. The amphitheaters' adult companies included both adult men, who played the male roles, and boys, who played the female roles; the private, or indoor, theater companies, on the other hand, were entirely composed of boys aged about 8 to 16, who were, or could pretend to be, candidates for singers in a church or a royal boys' choir. (Until 1660, professional theatrical companies included no women.) The playing space would appear much more familiar to modern audiences than the long-vanished amphitheaters; the later indoor theaters were, in fact, the ancestors of the typical modern theater. They were enclosed spaces, usually rectangular, with the stage filling one end of the rectangle and the audience arrayed in seats or benches across (and sometimes lining) the building's longer axis. These spaces staged plays less frequently than the public theaters (perhaps only once a week) and held far fewer spectators than the amphitheaters: about 200 to 600, as opposed to 2,500 or more. Fewer patrons mean a smaller gross income, unless each pays more. Not surprisingly, then, private theaters charged higher prices than the amphitheaters, probably sixpence, as opposed to a penny for the cheapest entry.

Protected from the weather, the indoor theaters presented plays later in the day than the amphitheaters, and used artificial illumination – candles in sconces or candelabra. But candles melt, and need replacing, snuffing, and trimming, and these practical requirements may have been part of the reason the indoor theaters introduced breaks in the performance, the intermission so dear to the heart of theatergoers and to the pocketbooks of theater concessionaires ever since. Whether motivated by the need to tend to the candles or by the entrepreneurs' wishing to sell oranges and liquor, or both, the indoor theaters eventually established the modern convention of the noncontinuous performance. In the early modern "private" theater, musical performances apparently filled the intermissions, which in Stuart theater jargon seem to have been called "acts."

At the end of the first decade of the seventeenth century, the distinction between public amphitheaters and private indoor companies ceased. For various cultural, political, and economic reasons, individual companies gained control of both the public, open-air theaters and the indoor ones, and companies mixing adult men and boys took over the formerly "private" theaters. Despite the death of the boys' companies and of their highly innovative theaters (for which such luminous playwrights as Ben Jonson, George Chapman, and John Marston wrote), their playing spaces and conventions had an immense impact on subsequent plays: not merely for the intervals (which stressed the artistic and architectonic importance of "acts"), but also because they introduced political and social satire as a popular dramatic ingredient, even in tragedy, and a wider range of actorly effects, encouraged by their more intimate playing spaces.

Even the briefest sketch of the Shakespearean theatrical world would be incomplete without some comment on the social and cultural dimensions of theaters and playing in the period. In an intensely hierarchical and status-conscious society, professional actors and their ventures had hardly any respectability; as we have indicated, to protect themselves against laws designed to curb vagabondage and the increase of masterless men, actors resorted to the near-fiction that they were the servants of noble masters, and wore their distinctive livery. Hence the company for which Shakespeare wrote in the 1590s called itself the Lord Chamberlain's Men and pretended that the public, money-getting performances were in fact rehearsals for private performances before that high court official. From 1598, the Privy Council had licensed theatrical companies, and after 1603, with the accession of King James I, the companies gained explicit royal protection, just as the Queen's Men had for a time under Queen Elizabeth. The Chamberlain's Men became the King's Men, and the other companies were patronized by the other members of the royal family.

These designations were legal fictions that half-concealed an important economic and social development, the evolution away from the theater's organization on the model of the guild, a self-regulating confraternity of individual artisans, into a proto-capitalist organization. Shakespeare's company became a joint-stock company, where persons who supplied capital and, in some cases, such as Shakespeare's, capital and talent, employed themselves and others in earning a return on that capital. This development meant that actors and theater companies were outside both the traditional guild structures, which required some form of civic or royal charter, and the feudal household organization of master-and-servant. This anomalous, maverick social and economic condition made theater companies practically unruly and potentially even dangerous; consequently, numerous official bodies – including the London metropolitan and ecclesiastical authorities as well as, occasionally, the royal court itself – tried, without much success, to control and even to disband them.

Public officials had good reason to want to close the theaters: they were attractive nuisances – they drew often riotous crowds, they were always noisy, and they could be politically offensive and socially insubordinate. Until the Civil War, however, anti-theatrical forces failed to shut down professional theater, for many reasons – limited surveillance and few police powers, tensions or outright hostilities among the agencies that sought to check or channel theatrical activity, and lack of clear policies for control. Another reason must have been the theaters' undeniable popularity. Curtailing any activity enjoyed by such a substantial percentage of the population was difficult, as various Roman emperors attempting to limit circuses had learned, and the Tudor-Stuart audience was not merely large, it was socially diverse and included women. The prevalence of public entertainment in this period has been underestimated. In fact, fairs, holidays, games, sporting events, the equivalent of modern parades, freak shows, and street exhibitions all abounded, but the theater was the most widely and frequently available entertainment to which people of every class had access. That fact helps account both for its quantity and for the fear and anger it aroused.

WILLIAM SHAKESPEARE OF
STRATFORD-UPON-AVON, GENTLEMAN

Many people have said that we know very little about William Shakespeare's life – pinheads and postcards are often mentioned as appropriately tiny surfaces on which to record the available information. More imaginatively and perhaps more correctly, Ralph Waldo Emerson wrote, "Shakespeare is the only biographer of Shakespeare. . . . So far from Shakespeare's being the least known, he is the one person in all modern history fully known to us."

In fact, we know more about Shakespeare's life than we do about almost any other English writer's of his era. His last will and testament (dated March 25, 1616) survives, as do numerous legal contracts and court documents involving Shakespeare as principal or witness, and parish records in Stratford and London. Shakespeare appears quite often in official records of King James's royal court, and of course Shakespeare's name appears on numerous title pages and in the written and recorded words of his literary contemporaries Robert Greene, Henry Chettle, Francis Meres, John Davies of Hereford, Ben Jonson, and many others. Indeed, if we make due allowance for the bloating of modern, run-of-the-mill bureaucratic records, more information has survived over the past four hundred years about William Shakespeare of Stratford-upon-Avon, Warwickshire, than is likely to survive in the next four hundred years about any reader of these words.

What we do not have are entire categories of information – Shakespeare's private letters or diaries, drafts and revisions of poems and plays, critical prefaces or essays, commendatory verse for other writers' works, or instructions guiding his fellow actors in their performances, for instance – that we imagine would help us understand and appreciate his surviving writings. For all we know, many such data never existed as written records. Many literary and theatrical critics, not knowing what might once have existed, more or less cheerfully accept the situation; some even make a theoretical virtue of it by claiming that such data are irrelevant to understanding and interpreting the plays and poems.

So, what do we know about William Shakespeare, the man responsible for thirty-seven or perhaps more plays, more than 150 sonnets, two lengthy narrative poems, and some shorter poems?

While many families by the name of Shakespeare (or some variant spelling) can be identified in the English Midlands as far back as the twelfth century, it seems likely that the dramatist's grandfather, Richard, moved to Snitterfield, a town not far from Stratford-upon-Avon, sometime before 1529. In Snitterfield, Richard Shakespeare leased farmland from the very wealthy Robert Arden. By 1552, Richard's son John had moved to a large house on Henley Street in Stratford upon-Avon, the house that stands today as "The Birthplace." In Stratford, John Shakespeare traded as a glover, dealt in wool, and lent money at interest; he also served in a variety of civic posts, including "High Bailiff," the municipality's equivalent of mayor. In 1557, he married Robert Arden's youngest daughter, Mary. Mary and John had four sons – William was the oldest – and four daughters, of whom only Joan outlived her most celebrated sibling. William was baptized (an event entered in the Stratford parish church records) on April 26, 1564, and it has become customary, without any good factual support, to suppose he was born on April 23, which happens to be the feast day of Saint George, patron saint of England, and is also the date on which he died, in 1616. Shakespeare married Anne Hathaway in 1582, when he was eighteen and she was twenty-six; their first child was born five months later. It has been generally assumed that the marriage was enforced and subsequently unhappy, but these are only assumptions; it has been estimated, for instance, that up to one third of Elizabethan brides were pregnant when they married. Anne and William Shakespeare had three children: Susanna, who married a prominent local physician, John Hall; and the twins Hamnet, who died young in 1596, and Judith, who married Thomas Quiney – apparently a rather shady individual. The name Hamnet was unusual but not unique: he and his twin sister were named for their godparents, Shakespeare's neighbors Hamnet and Judith Sadler. Shakespeare's father died in 1601 (the year of *Hamlet*), and Mary Arden Shakespeare died in 1608 (the year of *Coriolanus*). William Shakespeare's last surviving direct descendant was his granddaughter Elizabeth Hall, who died in 1670.

Between the birth of the twins in 1585 and a clear reference to Shakespeare as a practicing London dramatist in Robert Greene's sensationalizing, satiric pamphlet, *Greene's Groatsworth of Wit* (1592), there is no record of where William Shakespeare was or what he was doing. These seven so-called lost years have been imaginatively filled by scholars and other students of Shakespeare: some think he traveled to Italy, or fought in the Low Countries, or studied law or medicine, or worked as an apprentice actor/writer, and so on to even more fanciful possibilities. Whatever the biographical facts for those "lost" years, Greene's nasty remarks in 1592 testify to professional envy and to the fact that Shakespeare already had a successful career in London. Speaking to his fellow playwrights, Greene warns both generally and specifically:

> . . . trust them [actors] not: for there is an upstart crow, beautified with our feathers, that with his tiger's heart wrapped in a player's hide supposes he is as well able to bombast out a blank verse as the best of you; and being an absolute Johannes Factotum, is in his own conceit the only Shake-scene in a country.

The passage mimics a line from *3 Henry VI* (hence the play must have been performed before Greene wrote) and seems to say that "Shake-scene" is both actor and play-wright, a jack-of-all-trades. That same year, Henry Chettle protested Greene's remarks in *Kind-Heart's Dream,* and each of the next two years saw the publication of poems – *Venus and Adonis* and *The Rape of Lucrece,* respectively – publicly ascribed to (and dedicated by) Shakespeare. Early in 1595 he was named one of the senior members of a prominent acting company, the Lord Chamberlain's Men, when they received payment for court performances during the 1594 Christmas season.

Clearly, Shakespeare had achieved both success and reputation in London. In 1596, upon Shakespeare's application, the College of Arms granted his father the now-familiar coat of arms he had taken the first steps to obtain almost twenty years before, and in 1598, John's son – now permitted to call himself "gentleman" – took a 10 percent share in the new Globe playhouse. In 1597, he bought a substantial bourgeois house, called New Place, in Stratford – the garden remains, but Shakespeare's house, several times rebuilt, was torn down in 1759 – and over the next few years Shakespeare spent large sums buying land and making other investments in the town and its environs. Though he worked in London, his family remained in Stratford, and he seems always to have considered Stratford the home he would eventually return to. Something approaching a disinterested appreciation of Shakespeare's popular and professional status appears in Francis Meres's *Palladis Tamia* (1598), a not especially imaginative and perhaps therefore persuasive record of literary reputations. Reviewing contemporary English writers, Meres lists the titles of many of Shakespeare's plays, including one not now known, *Love's Labor's Won,* and praises his "mellifluous & hony-tongued" "sugred Sonnets," which were then circulating in manuscript (they were first collected in 1609). Meres describes Shakespeare as "one of the best" English playwrights of both comedy and tragedy. In *Remains . . . Concerning Britain* (1605),

William Camden – a more authoritative source than the imitative Meres – calls Shakespeare one of the "most pregnant witts of these our times" and joins him with such writers as Chapman, Daniel, Jonson, Marston, and Spenser. During the first decades of the seventeenth century, publishers began to attribute numerous play quartos, including some non-Shakespearean ones, to Shakespeare, either by name or initials, and we may assume that they deemed Shakespeare's name and supposed authorship, true or false, commercially attractive.

For the next ten years or so, various records show Shakespeare's dual career as playwright and man of the theater in London, and as an important local figure in Stratford. In 1608-9 his acting company – designated the "King's Men" soon after King James had succeeded Queen Elizabeth in 1603 – rented, refurbished, and opened a small interior playing space, the Blackfriars theater, in London, and Shakespeare was once again listed as a substantial sharer in the group of proprietors of the playhouse. By May 11, 1612, however, he describes himself as a Stratford resident in a London lawsuit – an indication that he had withdrawn from day-to-day professional activity and returned to the town where he had always had his main financial interests. When Shakespeare bought a substantial residential building in London, the Blackfriars Gatehouse, close to the theater of the same name, on March 10, 1613, he is recorded as William Shakespeare "of Stratford upon Avon in the county of Warwick, gentleman," and he named several London residents as the building's trustees. Still, he continued to participate in theatrical activity: when the new Earl of Rutland needed an allegorical design to bear as a shield, or *impresa,* at the celebration of King James's Accession Day, March 24, 1613, the earl's accountant recorded a payment of 44 shillings to Shakespeare for the device with its motto.

For the last few years of his life, Shakespeare evidently

concentrated his activities in the town of his birth. Most of the final records concern business transactions in Stratford, ending with the notation of his death on April 23, 1616, and burial in Holy Trinity Church, Stratford-upon-Avon.

THE QUESTION OF AUTHORSHIP

The history of ascribing Shakespeare's plays (the poems do not come up so often) to someone else began, as it continues, peculiarly. The earliest published claim that someone else wrote Shakespeare's plays appeared in an 1856 article by Delia Bacon in the American journal *Putnam's Monthly* – although an Englishman, Thomas Wilmot, had shared his doubts in private (even secretive) conversations with friends near the end of the eighteenth century. Bacon's was a sad personal history that ended in madness and poverty, but the year after her article, she published, with great difficulty and the bemused assistance of Nathaniel Hawthorne (then United States Consul in Liverpool, England), her *Philosophy of the Plays of Shakspere Unfolded.* This huge, ornately written, confusing farrago is almost unreadable; sometimes its intents, to say nothing of its arguments, disappear entirely beneath near-raving, ecstatic writing. Tumbled in with much supposed "philosophy" appear the claims that Francis Bacon (from whom Delia Bacon eventually claimed descent), Walter Ralegh, and several other contemporaries of Shakespeare's had written the plays. The book had little impact except as a ridiculed curiosity.

Once proposed, however, the issue gained momentum among people whose conviction was the greater in proportion to their ignorance of sixteenth- and seventeenth-century English literature, history, and society. Another American amateur, Catherine P. Ashmead Windle, made the next influential contribution to the cause when she published *Report to the British Museum* (1882), wherein she promised to open "the Cipher of Francis Bacon," though what she mostly offers, in the words of S. Schoenbaum, is "demented allegorizing." An entire new cottage industry grew from Windle's suggestion that the texts contain hidden, cryptographically discoverable ciphers – "clues" – to their authorship; and today there are not only books devoted to the putative ciphers, but also pamphlets, journals, and newsletters.

Although Baconians have led the pack of those seeking a substitute Shakespeare, in *"Shakespeare" Identified* (1920), J. Thomas Looney became the first published "Oxfordian" when he proposed Edward de Vere, seventeenth earl of Oxford, as the secret author of Shakespeare's plays. Also for Oxford and his "authorship" there are today dedicated societies, articles, journals, and books. Less popular candidates – Queen Elizabeth and Christopher Marlowe among them – have had adherents, but the movement seems to have divided into two main contending factions, Baconian and Oxfordian. (For further details on all the candidates for "Shakespeare," see S. Schoenbaum, *Shakespeare's Lives,* 2nd ed., 1991.)

The Baconians, the Oxfordians, and supporters of other candidates have one trait in common – they are snobs. Every pro-Bacon or pro-Oxford tract sooner or later claims that the historical William Shakespeare of Stratford-upon-Avon could not have written the plays because he could not have had the training, the university education, the experience, and indeed the imagination or background their author supposedly possessed. Only a learned genius like Bacon or an aristocrat like Oxford could have written such fine plays. (As it happens, lucky male children of the middle class had access to better education than most aristocrats in Elizabethan England – and Oxford was not particularly well educated.) Shakespeare received in the Stratford grammar school a formal education that would daunt many college graduates today; and popular rival playwrights such as the very learned Ben Jonson and George Chapman, both of whom also lacked university training, achieved great artistic success, without being taken as Bacon or Oxford.

Besides snobbery, one other quality characterizes the authorship controversy: lack of evidence. A great deal of testimony from Shakespeare's time shows that Shakespeare wrote Shakespeare's plays and that his contemporaries recognized them as distinctive and distinctly superior. (Some of that contemporary evidence is collected in E. K. Chambers, *William Shakespeare: A Study of Facts and Problems,* 2 vols., 1930.) Since that testimony comes from Shakespeare's enemies and theatrical competitors as well as from his co-workers and from the Elizabethan equivalent of literary journalists, it seems unlikely that, if any of these sources had known he was a fraud, they would have failed to record that fact.

Books About Shakespeare's Theater

Useful scholarly studies of theatrical life in Shakespeare's day include: G. E. Bentley, *The Jacobean and Caroline Stage,* 7 vols. (1941–68), and the same author's *The Professions of Dramatist and Player in Shakespeare's Time, 1590–1642* (1986); E. K. Chambers, *The Elizabethan Stage,* 4 vols. (1923); R. A. Foakes, *Illustrations of the English Stage, 1580–1642* (1985); Andrew Gurr, *The Shakespearean Stage,* 3rd ed. (1992), and the same author's *Play-going in Shakespeare's London,* 2nd ed. (1996); Edwin Nungezer, *A Dictionary of Actors* (1929); Carol Chillington Rutter, ed., *Documents of the Rose Playhouse* (1984).

Books About Shakespeare's Life

The following books provide scholarly, documented accounts of Shakespeare's life: G. E. Bentley, *Shakespeare: A Biographical Handbook* (1961); E. K. Chambers, *William Shakespeare: A Study of Facts and Problems,* 2 vols. (1930); S. Schoenbaum, *William Shakespeare: A Compact*

Documentary Life (1977); and *Shakespeare's Lives,* 2nd ed. (1991), by the same author. Many scholarly editions of Shakespeare's complete works print brief compilations of essential dates and events. References to Shakespeare's works up to 1700 are collected in C. M. Ingleby et al., *The Shakespeare Allusion-Book,* rev. ed., 2 vols. (1932).

The Texts of Shakespeare

As far as we know, only one manuscript conceivably in Shakespeare's own hand may (and even this is much disputed) exist: a few pages of a play called *Sir Thomas More*, which apparently was never performed. What we do have, as later readers, performers, scholars, students, are printed texts. The earliest of these survive in two forms: quartos and folios. Quartos (from the Latin for "four") are small books, printed on sheets of paper that were then folded twice, to make four leaves or eight pages. When these were bound together, the result was a squarish, eminently portable volume that sold for the relatively small sum of sixpence (translating in modern terms to about $5.00). In folios, on the other hand, the sheets are folded only once, in half, producing large, impressive volumes taller than they are wide. This was the format for important works of philosophy, science, theology, and literature (the major precedent for a folio Shakespeare was Ben Jonson's *Works*, 1616). The decision to print the works of a popular playwright in folio is an indication of how far up on the social scale the theatrical profession had come during Shakespeare's lifetime. The Shakespeare folio was an expensive book, selling for between fifteen and eighteen shillings, depending on the binding (in modern terms, from about $150 to $180). Twenty Shakespeare plays of the thirty-seven that survive first appeared in quarto, seventeen of which appeared during Shakespeare's lifetime; the rest of the plays are found only in folio.

The First Folio was published in 1623, seven years after Shakespeare's death, and was authorized by his fellow actors, the co-owners of the King's Men. This publication was certainly a mark of the company's enormous respect for Shakespeare; but it was also a way of turning the old plays, most of which were no longer current in the playhouse, into ready money (the folio includes only Shakespeare's plays, not his sonnets or other nondramatic verse). Whatever the motives behind the publication of the folio, the texts it preserves constitute the basis for almost all later editions of the playwright's works. The texts, however, differ from those of the earlier quartos, sometimes in minor respects but often significantly – most strikingly in the two texts of *King Lear,* but also in important ways in *Hamlet, Othello,* and *Troilus and Cressida.* (The variants are recorded in the textual notes to each play in the new Pelican series.) The differences in these texts represent, in a sense, the essence of theater: the texts of plays were initially not intended for publication. They were scripts, designed for the actors to perform – the principal life of the play at this period was in performance. And it follows that in Shakespeare's theater the playwright typically had no say either in how his play was performed or in the disposition of his text – he was an employee of the company. The authoritative figures in the theatrical enterprise were the shareholders in the company, who were for the most part the major actors. They decided what plays were to be done; they hired the playwright and often gave him an outline of the play they wanted him to write. Often, too, the play was a collaboration: the company would retain a group of writers, and parcel out the scenes among them. The resulting script was then the property of the company, and the actors would revise it as they saw fit during the course of putting it on stage. The resulting text belonged to the company. The playwright had no rights in it once he had been paid. (This system survives largely intact in the movie industry, and most of the playwrights of Shakespeare's time were as anonymous as most screenwriters are today.) The script could also, of course, continue to change as the tastes of audiences and the requirements of the actors changed. Many – perhaps most – plays were revised when they were reintroduced after any substantial absence from the repertory, or when they were performed by a company different from the one that originally commissioned the play.

Shakespeare was an exceptional figure in this world because he was not only a shareholder and actor in his company, but also its leading playwright – he was literally his own boss. He had, moreover, little interest in the publication of his plays, and even those that appeared during his lifetime with the authorization of the company show no signs of any editorial concern on the part of the author. Theater was, for Shakespeare, a fluid and supremely responsive medium – the very opposite of the great classic canonical text that has embodied his works since 1623.

The very fluidity of the original texts, however, has meant that Shakespeare has always had to be edited. Here is an example of how problematic the editorial project inevitably is, a passage from the most famous speech in *Romeo and Juliet,* Juliet's balcony soliloquy beginning "O Romeo, Romeo, wherefore art thou Romeo?" Since the eighteenth century, the standard modern text has read,

> What's Montague? It is nor hand, nor foot,
> Nor arm, nor face, nor any other part
> Belonging to a man. O be some other name!
> What's in a name? That which we call a rose
> By any other name would smell as sweet.
> > (II.2.40–44)

Editors have three early texts of this play to work from, two quarto texts and the folio. Here is how the First Quarto (1597) reads:

> Whats *Mountague?* It is nor band nor foote,
> Nor arme,nor face, nor any other part.
> Whats in a name? That which we call a Rose,
> By any other name would smell as sweet:

Here is the Second Quarto (1599):

> Whats *Mountague?* it is nor hand nor foote,
> Nor arme nor face, ô be some other name
> Belonging to a man.
> Whats in a name that which we call a rose,
> By any other word would smell as sweete,

And here is the First Folio (1623):

> What's *Mountague?* it is nor hand nor foote,
> Nor arme,nor face,O be some other name
> Belonging to a man.
> What? in a names that which we call a Rose,
> By any other word would smell as sweete,

There is in fact no early text that reads as our modern text does – and this is the most famous speech in the play. Instead, we have three quite different texts, all of which are clearly some version of the same speech, but none of which seems to us a final or satisfactory version. The transcendently beautiful passage in modern editions is an editorial invention: editors have succeeded in conflating and revising the three versions into something we recognize as great poetry. Is this what Shakespeare "really" wrote? Who can say? What we can say is that Shakespeare always had performance, not a book, in mind.

Books About the Shakespeare Texts

The standard study of the printing history of the First Folio is W. W. Greg, *The Shakespeare First Folio* (1955). J. K. Walton, *The Quarto Copy for the First Folio of Shakespeare* (1971), is a useful survey of the relation of the quartos to the folio. The second edition of Charlton Hinman's *Norton Facsimile* of the First Folio (1996), with a new introduction by Peter Blayney, is indispensable. Stanley Wells, Gary Taylor, John Jowett, and William Montgomery, *William Shakespeare: A Textual Companion,* keyed to the Oxford text, gives a comprehensive survey of the editorial situation for all the plays and poems.

THE GENERAL EDITORS

Introduction

WHY HAS *OTHELLO* always stood slightly apart from the other tragedies generally acknowledged to be among Shakespeare's supreme achievements? Regularly grouped with *Hamlet, King Lear,* and *Macbeth,* it is sometimes described as the most dramatic, the most playable, of the great tragedies, but such praise often masks a dubious assessment of its artistic status. Even those who most admire it, however, agree that *Othello* exhibits distinctive qualities that separate it from its dramatic kin. First, its title character is different. The Moor of Venice differs conspicuously from the other tragic heroes, differs from the English audience for which he was created, differs from the rest of the cast of *Othello.* The playwright takes pains to depict Othello as the alien whose strangeness is both fascinating and threatening. Second, the play's subject is unusual for tragedy, neither a struggle for control of the state nor a study of ancient heroism nor royal biography. Rather, *Othello* is about love – its beauty, its fragility, its vulnerability to hate. The passions represented seem private or perhaps narrow, not historically momentous. Here the battle for power is domestic, emotional, and personal.

George Bernard Shaw, commenting on Verdi's operatic version, mischievously remarked that "instead of *Otello* being an Italian opera written in the style of Shakespeare, *Othello* is a play written by Shakespeare in the style of Italian opera. It is quite peculiar among his works in this respect . . . and the plot is a pure farce plot." Shaw's flippant analysis is not atypical. Othello and *Othello* are distinctive in having earned the condescension, even scorn, of certain eloquent critics, from Thomas Rymer in the seventeenth century to F. R. Leavis and T. S. Eliot in the twentieth.

Rymer belittled the play's pretensions to tragic grandeur, lampooning it as a sign of what happens when "Maidens of quality . . . run away with Blackamoors." Eliot pitilessly complained that in the final, lyrical speech before his suicide Othello was "thinking about himself," "endeavouring to escape reality," and merely "cheering himself up."

It is doubtful that such reactions would have surprised the playwright. Shakespeare must have known that audiences would find his exotic hero unsettling, and he must have wanted it that way. So many of his dramatic choices in *Othello* seem original or surprising that they imply a deliberate effort to frustrate the expectations of the audience. All tragedy, of course, depends upon the confounding of expectation, and playwrights from Aeschylus forward have prized and magnified the ironies of a spectacular reversal of fortune. But in choosing and adapting a short story about a foolish captain who murders his wife, a tale first published in Italian by Giraldo Cinthio in 1565, Shakespeare has repeatedly made the difficult, the original choice. In the nature of his hero, the presentation of his villain, the addition and deepening of the minor figures, the pace of the action, the metadramatic layering, the risky reference to the staples of comedy – in each of these important respects, as in lesser ones, he has sought the unexpected effect. Examined in theatrical and historical context, *Othello* emerges as the product of an artistic imagination enlarging the boundaries of the theatrical medium, overturning conventions but using the spectator's familiarity with those conventions to intensify the force of their rejection. And placed in the context of its creator's career, the play becomes a skeptical review of his own ten-year commitment to the affirmations of comedy and the benefits of theatrical illusion.

Discussion of tragedy often begins with a treatment of the hero, and here such a procedure is especially appropriate because the play seems to demand immediate attention to its characters. For the twenty-first-century reader or playgoer, particularly in America, the problem of race is likely to be the primary consideration. This is a normal response, since every perceiver brings to every work of art a distinctive set of cultural determinants, an internalized batch of assumptions, opinions, blind spots, and wishes. That personal response should not be dismissed, since readers today cannot ignore the cultural centrality of race and its associated social and moral problems – slavery, oppression, intolerance, resentment, prejudice, and class conflict. Present concerns should be supplemented, however, with an awareness of the theatrical, historical, and cultural conditions obtaining when the play was written and first performed. To do so is not to suppress our own reactions or to minimize the play's relevance to current social or ethical issues. It is, rather, to understand our own reactions better by examining what the work might have meant to an earlier, different generation of people. Absorbing the prominent strain of black and white imagery in the text, our consciousness of race probably prompts us to think of the title character as an African, specifically a sub-Saharan African. This is how he is usually played in the modern theater. To the audience at the Globe, however, Othello's origins and appearance were probably less definite.

The Tragedy of Othello the Moor of Venice. It is worth pondering the distinctive mixture of associations the folio title would have ignited in the early modern mind. "Othello" is an unusual name, apparently a Shakespearean coinage (his counterpart in the source is unnamed). It sounds exotic or at least Mediterranean, deriving perhaps from an existing Italian name, "Otello," and (perhaps also) suggesting the North African "Otho" or "Othoman" or "Ottoman." Even stranger is the combination of locative nouns that follows the name, suggesting inconsistency, hybridity, the crossing of cultures. To begin with "Moor," the *Oxford English Dictionary* is of some help. In the ancient world, a Moor was

> a native of Mauretania, a region of Northern Africa corresponding to parts of Morocco and Algeria. In later times, one belonging to the people of mixed Berber and Arab race, Muslim in religion, who constitute the bulk of the population of North-western Africa, and who in the 8th c. conquered Spain. In the Middle Ages, and as late as the 17th c., the Moors were commonly supposed to be mostly black or very swarthy (though the existence of "white Moors" was recognized), and hence the word was often used for "negro"; cf. BLACKAMOOR.

Clearly the noun has meant different things to different people in different cultures at different times. The disparity between fact and opinion ("commonly supposed") is implicit here, even the disparity between opinions ("commonly supposed to be mostly black . . . though the existence of 'white Moors' was recognized"). When Iago disparages Othello as "a Barbary horse," he identifies him with the North African Muslim nation of Barbary, home of the Berbers. But the Moor has left his homeland and is now employed by the Duke of Venice, a city with a definite reputation in the seventeenth century. Venice was a hybrid, a metropolis on the Italian peninsula and yet a separate republic with widespread economic interests; unquestionably it was one of the centers of European civilization. Yet various texts of the period (e.g., Ben Jonson's *Volpone*) attest to the English opinion of Venice as dangerous and alluring, and indeed throughout the world the city was famous for its courtesans, its sophistication and potential treachery, its mystery. Shakespeare's Venetian senators are nobody's fools – they instantly penetrate the Turks' nautical trick (I.3) – and Iago, when he impugns

Desdemona's fidelity, summons up images of the notoriously duplicitous Venetian female. The sum of these conflicting signals is that none of the nouns in the title – not even "Tragedy" – is stable or plain in its signification.

Was Shakespeare's Othello black? The question itself demands interrogation, specifically the word "black." In twenty-first-century terms, the answer is "no." Othello was first acted by Richard Burbage, the principal tragedian of the King's Men, who played Richard III and probably Hamlet; he is unlikely to have resembled what would today be considered an African. But in early modern terms, the answer could be some form of "yes." The Elizabethan ideal of human beauty was what was called "fair," meaning light skin and either light brown or blond hair. Its opposite, the brunet, or person with darker skin or black hair, was known as "black" or "dark." Desdemona distinguishes, in her banter with Iago upon landing at Cyprus, between the "fair" (or blond) woman and the "black" (or dark) woman. Such definitions are also pertinent to the identity of the "Dark Lady" of Shakespeare's sonnets, "a woman colored ill" (Sonnet 144). In other words, Burbage's physical appearance may have been sufficiently "dark" or "black" to prompt, or at least to correspond to, the trait's development in Shakespeare's text.

Throughout the first scene Iago and Roderigo trade racist insults about Othello: "thick-lips," "lascivious Moor," "old black ram," "Barbary horse." But since these epithets proceed from hatred, which tends to foster caricature, they are not reliable guides to appearance. Burbage might have worn cork makeup to appear swarthy or ostensibly African: at court in 1605, Queen Anne and her ladies applied burnt cork to their faces and forearms when they performed in Jonson's *Masque of Blackness*. The question of this Moor's identity is further muddled by the matter of dress: since the London theater companies were known for impressive costumes, we might suppose that robes or other distinctive clothing might have been used to suggest Othello's lineage. But it is just as likely, given his profession, that Othello was dressed as a Venetian general. Or, considering the sketchy evidence about costuming on the early modern stage, Burbage's Moor may also have looked something like a Londoner, in doublet and hose. All of these qualifications and inconsistencies suggest that we cannot know exactly what Shakespeare's audience would have assumed about Othello's race.

In fact, we cannot know what Shakespeare's audience thought about the question of "race" at all. Categories of nationality and ethnicity in Shakespeare's England seem to have been more fluid than we are inclined to think or at least not to have existed in the relatively definite forms that obtain today. People recognized different racial characteristics and national types, of course, and these were often the source of prejudice. Queen Elizabeth signed a proclamation to deport some eighty-nine "Negroes and Blackamoors," at least partly because they were taking work away from native-born Englishmen: the text of the order refers repeatedly to "people of that kind." Othello's "kind" is entangled with the similarly complex matter of social station. Shakespeare has taken pains to emphasize the Moor's aristocratic roots – "I fetch my life and being / From men of royal siege [rank]" (I.2.21-22) – to insist that in global terms his status is no less exalted than that of Desdemona and her father. The effectiveness of his effort is illustrated in the writing of Charles Gildon, a critic who in 1694 published a passionate refutation of Thomas Rymer's bigoted analysis:

There is no reason in the nature of things why a *Negro* of equal Birth and Merit should not be on an equal bottom with a *German, Hollander, Frenchman,* &c. . . . *Othello* being of *Royal Blood* and a Christian, where is the disparity of the Match? If either side is advanc'd, 'tis *Desdemona.*

Gildon's views on race and intermarriage, probably not what we would expect from a late-seventeenth-century Englishman, attest to the difficulty of safely generalizing about early modern audiences' responses to Othello.

We may confidently declare, however, that a Moor was not an obvious choice as the hero of a tragedy circa 1604. Many Londoners had seen Africans in their city, owing to increased commerce with the southern hemisphere and the West Indies, and Elizabeth received an ambassador and his retinue from the King of Barbary in 1600 and 1601. This envoy may even have seen the performances by the Lord Chamberlain's Men at court during his stay; more to the point, they (and their principal playwright) may have seen him. Many Londoners had seen Moors on the stage in the 1590s, notably in plays by George Peele and Christopher Marlowe, and in the collaborative *Lust's Dominion* (1600). Shakespeare himself had already depicted two. In *Titus Andronicus*, Aaron is the wicked accomplice of Tamora, vicious Queen of the Goths; to the Elizabethan spectator, the darkness of his skin denoted the impurity of his soul. The physical appearance of the Prince of Morocco in *The Merchant of Venice* is not so explicitly described, although Portia sends him away with a swipe at his "complexion." As a rule Elizabethan playwrights employed their Moorish characters as manifestations of the Other, strangers or aliens whose obvious physical difference raised disturbing questions about community and nationhood, cultural difference, and unarticulated assumptions about social organization. In *The Merchant of Venice* the alien status of the Moroccan prince is matched by that of his Aragonian counterpart – in the 1590s Spaniards were often depicted as demonic – and by one of Shakespeare's most memorable and troubling outsiders, Shylock the Jew. These theatrical predecessors can often evoke derision, occasionally scorn, and sometimes even sympathy and respect from other characters and from the audience, but none displays the kind of charisma or invites exactly the degree of admiration that Othello inspires. The meaningful hybridity latent in the phrase "The Moor of Venice" is reflected in Othello's status as both stranger and hero.

This product of Shakespeare's audacity is one of the most original and enigmatic characters in world drama. Othello is a man of extremes, an African prince who has spent his life in "the tented field," without a permanent home. Now commissioned to lead the forces of Venice, Othello protects the republic's interests from the "Turks," the barbarians with whom he himself is identified by his enemies and, probably, by a portion of the audience. Early-seventeenth-century Europeans thought of Moors, Turks, and Africans as pagan, but Othello is a Christian, a baptized convert whose Christianity is an important marker of his assimilation into Venice and the values of "civilization." In his marriage to Desdemona, he has traded independence and the masculine realm of the battlefield for emotional commitment and feminine companionship. Accustomed to "feats of broils and battle," Othello is an alien in this realm of domesticity, and Iago will exploit his naïveté and diffidence about marriage and women generally. At the beginning of Act Two, the Venetians' sophisticated courtesies and badinage would seem to be predicated on Othello's absence. As soon as his ship lands at Cyprus, the verbal register changes drastically, from Cassio's praise of Desdemona as "a maid / That paragons description and wild fame" (II.1.61-62) to Othello's "O my fair warrior!" (181). The theatrical milieu further complicates the portrait, in that audiences are asked to reconcile the foreign and the familiar. At the first performances this manifestation of the Other was acted by the most famous tragedian in England, and *Othello* is rarely produced without a major player to take the title part. The strangeness of the character may distance us, but at the same time we are attracted by Othello's undeniable star quality.

All these incongruities are consistent with the conventions of tragedy. The tragic figure is usually constructed according to a paradox, as we know from *King Lear* – the king who is also a fool – and from *Hamlet* – the brilliant student for whom intelligence proves fatal. For centuries tragic playwrights have created powerful, charismatic men and women whose uncompromising faith in themselves is coupled with an indomitable will. They are devoted to their own subjective vision of the world and their place in it, and this commitment, reinforced by pride or what the Greeks called hubris, bestows upon them both great strength and great vulnerability. Antigone, with her unwavering moral resolution, *will* see her brother buried even at the cost of her own life. Oedipus *will* cleanse Thebes by finding and punishing the murderer within the gates. Tragic figures may be described as idealists, adhering to an elevated standard of conduct both admirable and impossible to sustain, and expecting such commitment from those around them. Always these men and women are absolutists, unwilling to bend their principles. As Helen Gardner puts it, "the tragic hero usurps the function of the gods and attempts to remake the world."*

Othello's distinctive vision is both a product and a guarantor of his military career: he is the veteran leader impatient with failure, unwilling to waver between alternatives, accustomed to seeing things – the pun is unavoidable in this play – in terms of black and white. Uncertainty has no place in his world; indeed, to a military man, it is potentially fatal. Thus his rhetorical ploy before the Senate, "little of this great world can I speak" (I.3.86), is, ironically, fatally true. Like Hamlet, like Lear, he is an innocent. But the simplicity of Othello's construction of reality, his Platonic sense of good and evil – "men should be what they seem" (III.3.128), and his intuitive, martial code of action should not obscure his ex-

* "The Noble Moor," *Proceedings of the British Academy,* 41 (1955): 201.

ceptionally fertile and sensitive imagination. This imaginative gift is one source of his charisma. It underwrites his narrative and rhetorical success, in that he knows what will impress his listeners, from Brabantio and Desdemona in their initial meetings, to his senatorial judges, to the crowd of onlookers at the tragic conclusion. He imagines and wills himself into a world of nobility and integrity, an ideal realm in which officers do not fail in their duty, wives do not misplace love tokens, evil can be recognized, attacked, and destroyed.

Othello's heroic status is conveyed chiefly by his rhetoric, a style of speech aptly called "the Othello music."* No one else in the play (or in any other play) speaks the way Othello does. His language is extravagant and exotic; it is the vehicle for conveying the narrative of his colorful, romantic past; it is the source of his personal attraction, the instrument that wins Desdemona's heart and assures his triumph over Brabantio before the signory. Although Othello professes ignorance of the subtleties of oratory – "Rude am I in my speech" (I.3.81) – that claim is a performative tactic. His defense of his marriage (I.3.76-170) is poetic, stirring, and rhetorically dazzling, a narrative of a narrative of narratives. Othello tells the senators (and the audience) the story of his telling Desdemona the stories of his life, and the romantic, beguiling style is built with the staples of poetry: colorful imagery ("tented field," "deserts idle"); poetic patterns founded on doubled consonants and vowels ("sold to slavery," "hills whose heads touch heaven"); repeated words, often at the beginning of lines ("of most disastrous chances, / Of moving accidents . . . Of hairbreadth scapes . . . Of being taken by the insolent foe"; "She gave . . . She swore . . . She wished . . . She thanked . . . She loved"); seductive rhythms grounded in repetition and formal balance ("Her

---

* This is the title of G. Wilson Knight's chapter on the play in *The Wheel of Fire* (Oxford: Oxford University Press, 1930).

father loved me, oft invited me, / Still questioned me the story of my life / From year to year"); exotic diction ("anthropophagi"). The speech comes to rest on a pair of gracefully poised lines, a sentence in which the symmetrical rhetoric captures the sympathy between the lovers and forbids objection: "She loved me for the dangers I had passed, / And I loved her that she did pity them." The Moor belongs in a very small class of extraordinary, distinctive speakers, including Falstaff, Hamlet, Macbeth, Cleopatra, and perhaps Coriolanus.

Othello's command of such expressive gifts not only makes him charismatic but also signifies extraordinary imaginative reach. In first greeting Desdemona on Cyprus, he sets their joyous reunion in a context of passion and fatal risk: "If after every tempest come such calms, / May the winds blow till they have wakened death!" (II.1.184-85). Such extremity characterizes the great aria in which Othello imagines Desdemona's infidelity as the immediate undoing of his world: "O, now forever / Farewell the tranquil mind!" (III.3.347-48). The soaring lament draws its poetic energy from its colorful images, the rhythms of reiterated words, the musical echo of repeated vowels, and other verbal patterns typical of this famously compelling voice. Audible through the middle of the third act, this heroic register serves as the benchmark for measuring the hero's tragic collapse, as we hear his language degenerate into the vulgar, misogynist, and even bestial style of Iago. The poetic extravagance sounds again in the last scene, now shaded with a cosmic despair: "Blow me about in winds! roast me in sulphur! / Wash me in steep-down gulfs of liquid fire!" (V.2.280-81). Relying on such flamboyant rhetoric to make his earthly exit, he conjures up "Arabian trees," "Their medicinable gum," and, "in Aleppo once, . . . a malignant and a turbaned Turk" (V.2.350-53). The powerful beauty of Othello's language is Shakespeare's instrument for delineating the contours of his heroic persona – courage, integrity, professional confidence, absolute commitment to duty, sacred faith in his wife. "Perdition catch my soul / But I do love thee! and when I love thee not, / Chaos is come again" (III.3.90-92): the patterns of those three lines reveal the connection between the exalted speech and the radically simplified conception of fidelity and love.

His verbal authority and charisma permit Othello to compete with his antagonist for theatrical authority. Iago is Shakespeare's third longest role, behind Hamlet and Richard III, and except for the eleven-line "scene" in which a herald reads a proclamation and the few private moments when Desdemona and Emilia prepare for bed, Iago is onstage in every scene. The role of Othello, while not so lengthy, still has more lines than any other of Shakespeare's tragic heroes except (again) Hamlet. The two major women's roles are distinctive and memorable also, and even Cassio appears in all but three scenes. This enumeration of lines and entrances helps to establish a major structural principle: Shakespeare has concentrated the audience's attention on these major figures, permitting no diversion or escape but requiring unrelieved scrutiny of this core group of characters. We come to know them as complex dramatic persons, but through them we are also allowed access to a realm beyond character. As Verdi put it in a letter written while he entertained the offer to compose *Otello,* "It is quite possible that [Shakespeare] might have come across a Falstaff of some kind; but it's most unlikely that he ever met a villain quite so villainous as Iago, and he could never have met women as angelic as Cordelia, Imogen, or Desdemona, etc. Yet they are so true."* As Verdi perceived, Shakespeare's Iago and Desdemona are so theatrically potent because they are carefully observed persons ("so true") who at the same

---

* Letter to Countess Clarina Maffei, October 20, 1876, quoted in Julian Budden, *The Operas of Verdi,* vol. 3 (New York: Oxford University Press, 1981), p. 317.

time stand symbolically for something beyond themselves ("villainous" / "angelic"). The composer's remarks also identify the antithetical method to which Shakespeare always subscribes, as well as the form of antithesis specific to this play, the contest between hell and heaven for the soul of the hero.

The symbolic method is epitomized in the two contestants struggling for possession of Othello: Iago and Desdemona. When *Othello* was first performed, the Tudor morality plays were still attracting English audiences (although in London they had mostly been superseded by more sophisticated fare), and those plays feature the temptation of the hero by two competing angels, the good and bad, or an angel and a devil. No doubt recalling Christopher Marlowe's evocation of the morality tradition a decade earlier, when a good angel and a bad angel counsel Doctor Faustus, Shakespeare explicitly associates his villain and heroine with this theatrical pattern. The plot takes the form of a *psychomachia,* a battle between angelic and demonic forces for spiritual control of the main character. Othello stands between his ensign ("ancient") and his wife; he moves, during the course of the third act, from Desdemona to Iago, from heaven to hell, from faith to depravity. In representing this movement the poet develops a network of terms and images that sustains our awareness of hell and demons, of a spiritually charged cosmic struggle. The word "heaven" is heard with exceptional frequency (although in some cases in the folio text it serves as a euphemism for the censored "God"). "Hell" (or some form of it) sounds more frequently in *Othello* than in any other play, and if, as may be the case, Shakespeare's actors pronounced the title character's name as "Ot-Hello," the demonic noun reverberates even more frequently and meaningfully.

The horrified onlookers recognize Iago as a demonic figure, a "hellish villain," at the play's end, but from the beginning Shakespeare depicts his methods as infernal, largely by means of the character's diction. In one of his first speeches Iago presents himself as a kind of anti-Creator, negating the biblical Yahweh's "I am what I am" in his "I am not what I am" (I.1.64). Iago ensnares Cassio with the aid of alcohol, personified several times as a "devil" that poisons the brain, and he intoxicates Othello's imagination by "pour[ing] . . . pestilence into his ear" (II.3.344). His sermon to the shamed Cassio is "Divinity of hell!" (II.3.338). The most striking manifestation of a demonic nature is Iago's profound hatred, a negative energy that expresses itself variously as envy, cynicism, and misogyny. In lecturing Roderigo on the need for self-restraint, he espouses a doctrine of fierce naturalism, reducing all human experience to the physical, the mechanistic. As he sings in the drinking song, "man's life's but a span" (II.3.67). Women in general are animalistic ("wildcats"); Venetian women in particular are deceitful and sexually voracious. Othello, like all Southern foreigners, is "changeable," "an erring barbarian." To Iago's ear the "Othello music" is no more than "bombast circumstance" (padded rhetoric) and "fantastical lies." Emotion and romantic sentiment he dismisses as ridiculous. The act of love, entirely without spiritual dimension, is merely bestial: "a lust of the blood and permission of the will," "the beast with two backs." Reason is the key to sanity and balance, says the sociopath.

As compelling as Iago is, Shakespeare gives him a worthy counterpart in Desdemona. Theatrically and tonally, her femininity makes her especially welcome in a play about soldiers in a military outpost. Her open simplicity counterbalances Iago's concealed perversion. This innocence appears in her candor before the Venetian Senate, when she politely but firmly defies her father and frankly confesses her physical and emotional attachment to her husband. It is most apparent in her naive pleading for Cassio. Shakespeare emphasizes her otherworldly purity by lingering over the bedtime chat between the two women (IV.3.10-104), a conversation in which Desdemona is shocked at Emilia's cavalier sexual code. Her unshakable devotion to her murderous husband, especially her effort to exonerate him by blaming herself with her last breath, has left many readers and spectators incredulous. But such unworldly innocence is a necessary pole in the symbolic structure of the play. Othello's "fair warrior" of Act Two becomes his "fair devil" of Act Three and then "false as hell" in Act Four. In the end, although the victory of evil is not total – Iago will be punished – the embodiment of good, the "heavenly true" Desdemona, lies mute and lifeless. The annihilation of such purity is a source of the play's tremendous emotional power, the effect that led Dr. Johnson to declare, "I am glad that I have ended my revisal of this dreadful scene. It is not to be endured."*

The clarity of Shakespeare's dramatic oppositions should not, however, blind us to the subtlety with which his characters are drawn. Onstage Iago's cloven foot is concealed, and Desdemona's halo a little tarnished. For one or two fleeting moments we are invited to feel Iago's pain at Othello's professional rejection of him: the hardworking veteran has been passed over in favor of the college boy. But most of the time his villainy is glaringly obvious to us and invisible to the rest of the cast. They see something quite different. "Honest Iago": Othello uses the epithet ten times, Cassio twice, and Desdemona once. Each of these references delivers an excruciating ironic charge, and a precondition of such an ironic effect is that the term be spoken innocently, without a hint of irony. To those around him, Iago is the blunt, reliable soldier, the helpful fellow to whom people routinely turn in time of crisis. Roderigo, Cassio, Desdemona, and Othello all confide in him and seek his aid. In Act Four, Iago prudently rebuffs Lodovico's confidential query at Othello's rage, as if to

---

* *The Works of Samuel Johnson,* ed. Arthur Sherbo (New Haven: Yale University Press, 1968), vol. 8, p. 1045.

preserve his reputation for discretion: "It is not honesty in me to speak / What I have seen and known" (IV.1.271-72). The amount of time we spend alone with Iago, the privileged view we get of his diseased mind, is calculated to repel us, and morally we are repelled; but such intimacy nevertheless creates an ironic affinity between villain and audience. Shakespeare links us to his villain by modifying the method developed for Richard III, and this theatrical attachment secures an intellectual bond that ensures complicity.

Shakespeare's presentation of Desdemona is just as complex and unusual. Innocent victim though she be, she is also a strong-willed, independent young woman, one who commands all the forms of courtliness and social repartee. But while it may pain us to admit it, this heroine is capable of surprising insensitivity, even hardheadedness. Having resolved to plead for the dismissed Cassio and to help restore him to Othello's favor, Desdemona neglects such vital conditions as context, timing, and reception. Or to put it less flatteringly, she makes herself into something of a pest. Despite her husband's reluctance and his manifest attempts at polite evasion – "Not now, sweet Desdemon; some other time. . . . No, not tonight" (III.3.55-57) – she perseveres in demanding to know when Othello will receive Cassio and hear his apology. That request, as she artlessly observes, is as much a favor to Othello as it is to Cassio, and yet in the tragic environment such innocent persistence, as Iago knows, is self-destructive and potentially fatal. Her oblivious innocence makes itself heard when, after Othello's brutal accusations, she unwittingly undermines her own purity of mind with an unconscious pun: "I cannot say 'whore.' / It does abhor me now I speak the word" (IV.2.161-62). As Iago admits, devils are adept at arranging "heavenly shows," and by the same ironic token it seems impossible that a poet with Shakespeare's ear, taking the name of his heroine from Cinthio's "Disdemona," failed to note the "demon" lurking in "the divine Desdemona."

This shading of character extends to the rest of the cast. The good-looking and fortunate Cassio not only has a weak head for wine, but the *veritas* released by the *vinum* discloses an unlovely vanity and arrogance about his rank, particularly a sense of entitlement. Even the gullible Roderigo attracts a moment of sympathy in his ignominious death. Emilia boldly defends Desdemona at the cost of her own life, but she is tainted by her lie about the handkerchief. Her defense of female desire and denunciation of masculine cruelty are exceedingly welcome when they finally come (IV.3), and yet she declares herself amenable to adultery under the right circumstances. Emilia's casual attitude toward infidelity helps also to complicate the character of the third woman in the cast. Although Iago calls Bianca a "whore," she seems to dote wholeheartedly on Cassio, and the significance of her name (*bianca*=white) not only complicates our reading of her character but enriches the imagistic texture of the play. When she protests to Emilia that she is "no strumpet, but of life as honest / As you that thus abuse me" (V.1.123-24), there may be some justice to the claim, given that we have just heard Emilia say she would sell her body for the right price. As the main plot makes clear, hasty judgments about who is a whore can be fatal.

The struggle for Othello's soul is swift and horrific, confined to a single dramatic unit known as the "Temptation Scene" (III.3). In the space of some 450 lines Iago pollutes Othello's imagination, separates him psychologically from his wife, and ensnares the hero's soul. Logic insists that the reversal is too fast, that Othello's surrender to jealous vengeance is not prepared, that such a change of heart in so short a time is impossible. Further, it may strike us as preposterous, as it did Rymer in the seventeenth century, that the fate of Desdemona should hang on something as trivial as a handkerchief, albeit a magical one. These would seem to be pitfalls that any novice in a creative writing course would have the sense to avoid. So rather than assume that Shakespeare didn't notice them, we should recognize that he courted such improbabilities, that he risked telling the story this way because speed and incredulity intensify the horrifying effect of the tragic turn. Critics long ago observed that he conceals the logical impossibilities of his plot by employing a double time scheme in *Othello*. The Venetians disembark at Cyprus during the day on Saturday, and Desdemona dies on Sunday night. By such a reckoning "a thousand" acts of sexual infidelity would seem unlikely. Yet Shakespeare condenses Othello's undoing into a single implausible episode so as to increase its affective power and enhance its meaning. Speed is an inevitable result of Othello's heroic absolutism – "To be once in doubt / Is once to be resolved" (III.3.179-80) – and the thematic significance of such swift destruction is incalculable. His refusal to compromise, his courage, and his decisiveness are the properties that have elevated him to high rank and led him to Desdemona, but these are the same qualities that destroy him. That is the nature of tragedy, or to quote Othello, "the pity of it."

That Iago tempts Othello to self-destruction almost entirely with words, words artfully arranged and brilliantly delivered, indicates that the villain's skills are precisely those of the playwright who created him. Lying may be regarded as a malicious form of fiction, and Iago's fictions require an acute sense of audience and mastery of histrionic and rhetorical techniques. His manipulation of Roderigo functions as a rehearsal for the more challenging assault on Othello, and he employs similar strategies in both schemes. In his endeavor to corrupt Othello's mind, Iago provokes curiosity by means of oblique statements ("I like not that," III.3.35) and provocative questions. He works his victim psychologically by flattering and then distancing him, pulling him in and pushing him away. One of his most efficient strategies is the appeal to stock characters – the cunning Venetian wife, the handsome seducer – that give Othello an intellectual purchase in the midst of chaos. Perhaps most impressively, Iago spins compelling stories teeming with vivid, salacious pictures, to which Othello's sensitive imagination responds immediately and ferociously:

> IAGO
>   Would you, the supervisor, grossly gape on?
>   Behold her topped?
> OTHELLO   Death and damnation! O!
>   (III.3.395-96)

As his scheme proceeds, Iago distributes his theatrical tactics in ascending order of effectiveness, and by the time he reaches "Cassio's dream" (419-26), that erotic fantasy of refracted pictures and mumbled words, he has reduced Othello's own verbal powers to exclamations and monosyllables: "O monstrous! monstrous!"; "O, blood, blood, blood!" Iago is also the master of detail, a gift revealed in his ability to create a weapon out of a preposition:

> OTHELLO   What? what?
> IAGO
>   Lie –
> OTHELLO   With her?
> IAGO   With her, on her; what you will.
>   (IV.1.33-34)

Iago supplements his dialogue with a single prop, the handkerchief, but it too is employed in a theatrical scenario. Cassio and Bianca unwittingly perform for Othello, with Iago as director of, actor in, and, a few minutes later, reviewer of the show. Finally, Iago knows his audience: he plays unerringly upon Othello's insecurities about his status as a non-Venetian, as a black man in a white world, as inexperienced in the ways of women.

It has been observed that tragedy when speeded up turns into comedy. By allowing Othello to succumb so quickly, Shakespeare has risked inviting a comic response to this deadly action, and a number of critics have accepted that invitation, notably Shaw with his remarks about the plot as "pure farce." That Othello has so often been smirked at or that *Othello* has evoked responses proper to comedy is perhaps not surprising. In his furious progress toward self-destruction Othello sometimes resembles a conventional figure of Renaissance comedy, in which sexual jealousy was a popular topic. The butt of the jokes was usually the insecure husband who wrongly mistrusts his wife and consumes himself with jealousy and doubt; eventually, however, some providential force dispels the confusion and happily reunites the virtuous wife and embarrassed husband. Shakespeare's fellow playwrights had created variations on this paranoid male, entertaining audiences with farcical stage business, frenzied language, and the rich theme of self-delusion, of an imagination run wild. In plays such as George Chapman's *All Fools* and John Marston's *What You Will* the foolish husband isolates himself in a realm of fantasy, dramatizing his misery in seamy images, hectoring his wife with sarcasm and rhetorical questions, often losing control of language altogether. Shakespeare himself had created such a buffoon several years earlier in *The Merry Wives of Windsor*.

The most colorful of these paranoid husbands appears in Ben Jonson's *Every Man in His Humour* (1598), a play Shakespeare himself had acted in. We cannot know whether or not his own experience on the comic stage prompted him to explore the tragic implications of sexual suspicion. Nor can we say whether he knew such impulses personally, as a biographical reading of the sonnets would suggest. In either or both cases, Shakespeare deliberately invokes the language, the imaginative delirium, and the furious motion of the comic type in his creation of Othello. Here is Jonson's suspicious husband, a paranoid merchant whose name, Thorello, must in this context be taken as significant:

> Who will not judge him worthy to be robbed,
> That sets his doors wide open to a thief
> And shows the felon where his treasure lies?
> Again, what earthy spirit but will attempt
> To taste the fruit of beauty's golden tree
> When leaden sleep seals up the dragon's eye?
> (*Every Man in His Humour,*
> quarto text, III.1.14–21)

A Jacobean audience would have been unlikely to miss Othello's appropriation of such language: the comic husband's metaphors of robbery, his rhetorical questions, his laments at being tortured by knowledge, his obsession with images of bestiality, his increasing misogyny, his fantasies of brutal revenge. "I found not Cassio's kisses on her lips. / He that is robbed, not wanting what is stol'n, / Let him not know't, and he's not robbed at all" (III.3.341–43): this wish for oblivion is only one of many moments when Othello's speech and thought intersect with those of his comic double. To an audience anticipating tragedy, recognition of such parallels must have been disorienting. Confronted with comic traits in a tragic environment, the spectator is tempted toward the conventional, scornful response and is baited with the false promise of resolution. But laughter is forestalled by the seriousness of the context and consciousness of the tragic mode, and providence fails to intervene. The tragic hero's descent into such unseemly behavior increases the depth and intensifies the significance of the tragic fall. In fact, the condescension Othello's behavior has evoked in critics over the centuries suggests that the playwright's audacious stroke was a success.

Shakespeare's identification of Othello with Thorello is one element in a comprehensive strategy: he has refitted the machinery of comedy to augment the tragic power of the play. (*Romeo and Juliet* is another tragedy that makes use of just such cues; similarly, the multiple versions of the Lear story, before Shakespeare took it up, end happily.) The dramatist frames the story of Othello as a comedy gone wrong, a look at what happens after the wedding banquet, Act Six of one of his romantic comedies. The first act resembles a comedy in miniature: the setting of the first two scenes, the street, is a convention not of tragedy but of Roman and Italian comedy. The action involves an elopement between a man and a young woman, a clever subordinate who serves the hero, a competitor for the hand of the bride, an irascible father seeking to undo the marriage, and a public recognition and sanction of the union. A veteran theatergoer might have noted the parallels with *Much Ado About Nothing* (1598), a comedy also derived from Italian sources: the "Italian" setting, a slandered bride, a conniving, hateful officer, and an irrational, inexperienced bridegroom. Even the journey to Cyprus, a dangerous and unstable island, famous as the birthplace of Venus, inverts the Shakespearean journey to a green world that fosters revelation and emotional reordering in the romantic comedies.

These comic affinities enrich Shakespeare's tragic representation by producing an unsparing critique of comic optimism. The correspondences are not exact, of course, and most pertain to the opening movement of the tragedy, but such comic staples invite familiar reactions that the playwright then foils by driving the narrative in a contrary direction. The resemblances of setting and character matter less than the meanings to which they contribute and the responses to which an audience is prompted. *Othello* is a penetrating examination of the nature of evil, particularly its destructive capacity in the realm of love. A precondition of appreciating that portrayal is recognizing Shakespeare's challenge to the affirmations that normally attend the comic ending.

Othello was performed at court on November 2, 1604, perhaps as a new play, perhaps new only to the new king. A scholarly effort to push composition of the play as far back as 1602 has reopened the question of its date, but wherever between 1602 and 1604 we place it, we must acknowledge that the tragedy appeared at a pivotal moment in Shakespeare's creative life. The five years between 1599 and 1604 represent an unsettled period in his artistic development, a phase that sees a transition from the comedies and histories that dominated his first decade to the tragedies and romances that characterized the second. A list of titles from this period, even though their precise chronology is uncertain, indicates the vast range of tonal emphasis: *As You Like It, Julius Caesar, Henry V, Hamlet, Twelfth Night, Troilus and Cressida, All's Well That Ends Well,* and *Measure for Measure.* Most of these plays display the characteristics of more than one dramatic mode. Structurally, *Henry V* is a comedy ending in a marriage, although the price of its "festive" conclusion is high. *Troilus* embodies a kind of formal impasse, poised between comedy and tragedy. In moving from comedy to tragedy, the playwright was testing permutations of the major dramatic modes, shading the comedies with potentially tragic insights and drawing upon comic contrasts in telling a tragic story. Whether *Othello* was written in the middle of this phase or even last in the sequence of works, it clearly partakes of and benefits from what might be called their tonal ambiguity or formal instability. Shakespeare seems to have been exploring the interdependence of comedy and tragedy, exploiting the effects of each mode to test their antithetical conceptions of experience. Tragedy investigates and represents the nature of evil by allowing glimpses of harmony and comic solution. Thus Shakespeare's repeated reference to comic convention sharpens the definition of evil by teasing the audience with intimations of its opposite.

The evil that haunts *Othello* is especially engrossing

because it is intimately related to Shakespeare's own livelihood. In telling a story of deception and revenge the playwright confronts the dangers of illusion, the malignancy of the imagination, the threat of theater itself. Imagination is the great affirmative faculty in most of his comedies, serving Petruchio and Rosalind and other well-meaning lovers and players as a creative, therapeutic, unifying force. *A Midsummer Night's Dream* is the playwright's defense of fantasy and, beyond that, his supreme apology for the stage. In the darkness of the Athenian wood, imagination is associated with dreams, vision, fantasy, fancy, fiction, and finally with love. It is a source of joy, of revelation, of access to the divine. In the last scene of *Dream,* the benighted Duke Theseus reflects condescendingly on the uses of imagination and associates it with the lunatic, the lover, and the poet. Some eight years after composing that derisive indictment, Shakespeare himself begins to take seriously the pernicious effects of the faculty that he has been accustomed to celebrate, confronting and criticizing the imaginative sources of his own art.

The turn to tragedy both results from and helps to nourish Shakespeare's growing anxiety about the fraudulence of theatricality and disgust at the ease with which the creative faculty may be abused. The mature comedies stage previews of this peril, as in *Twelfth Night,* where Malvolio confuses erotic fantasies with facts. But the tragic frame presents the consequences of the depraved or perverted imagination as fatal, not risible: in *Othello* creativity serves murder and revenge. Theseus's lunatic, lover, and poet all appear in *Othello,* albeit in fragmented and burlesqued forms. Narcissism is the only kind of love Iago displays, but he is both a poet, or maker of fictions, and a lunatic, a man whose imagination has poisoned him so that he takes pleasure in the invention and performance of malicious acts. Othello as lover is the key to the plot, of course, but he is also a spinner of tales whose own responsive imagination Iago manages to contaminate with filthy images, and by the fourth act he has descended into a kind of madness. Desdemona, too, is credited with imaginative insight. Not only does she respond empathetically to Othello's exotic tales, but she also "saw Othello's visage in his mind" (I.3.252): looking beyond the body to the heart and spirit, she loves so profoundly that she seems to legitimize Theseus's scornful remark about the lover's seeing "Helen's beauty in a brow of Egypt." The principal players, in other words, all embody or are associated with some aspect of the imagination, and they either misuse or are themselves abused by the very quality that Shakespeare had spent the first decade of his career affirming.

Othello may be read as an allegory of that career, a kind of artistic biography in which the brief symbiotic marriage of tragedy and comedy (in, say, *Troilus and Cressida* and *Measure for Measure*) comes to an end, and tragedy smothers comedy. According to this scenario, the part of the angry father is taken by Sir Philip Sidney, who had warned, in the *Apology for Poetry,* against dramatic miscegenation, against mixing the kings of tragedy and the clowns of comedy. But Shakespeare's rejection of the mixed form involves not just decorum but a philosophical metamorphosis. Increasingly conscious of the strength and ubiquity of evil in the mortal world, the playwright begins to distrust the representational fidelity of the comic mode and, artistically speaking, allows the suspicious and darker form to murder it. The subsequent tragedies, *King Lear, Timon of Athens,* and *Macbeth,* are among Shakespeare's most dispiriting works, somber expositions of the duplicity of theater and the danger of illusion as manifested in feigning daughters, flattering friends, equivocal witches. Comedy has very little place in these play-worlds. The comic cues and foils that function so ironically in *Othello* are striking because, for the next few years, Shakespeare banishes them from his drama. And then, turning from tragedy to romance, he will reverse the process, employing the structures and persons of tragedy to intensify the felicity of the comic or romantic ending.

Tragedy has proven a durable and esteemed form through the centuries because it raises profound questions, elicits meanings from serious stories, explores the mysteries of experience. To see *Othello* as a tale of jealousy as Rymer and others have done is to mistake a partial manifestation of the play's subject for the subject itself. Jealousy is an emotional symptom. The real subject of *Othello* is the fragility of love, its inability to survive the corrosive conditions of a tragic world. Likewise, Iago is not ultimately responsible for the tragedy: he supplies the weapon, but Othello uses it on himself. Shakespeare represents and permits the audience to savor the potential joys of human love – physical, emotional, spiritual – and then depicts the brutal self-destruction of those possibilities. Looking hard at human experience through the dark filter of tragedy, the playwright portrays the vulnerability of mortals, even the most gifted and accomplished, to the forces of hatred and fear within themselves.

If Othello's tragedy is the paradoxical self-annihilation of his imaginative talent, a trait that ought to be beneficent and consolatory, then it is hard not to see Shakespeare the artist as exploring his own distinctive vulnerability. At the same time, however, he could not have been unaware of the ironic triumph that the play itself constitutes, an imaginative tour de force about the hazards of the imagination. Perhaps it is troubling to read *Othello* as Shakespeare's self-indictment, and yet the corollary to that reading is the recognition that his self-scrutiny produced a work of art that still disturbs, moves, and even consoles us.

RUSS MCDONALD
University of North Carolina at Greensboro

Note on the Text

OTHELLO PRESENTS AN EDITOR with formidable textual problems. The play was first printed in quarto (Q) by Thomas Walkley in 1622, just a year before its appearance in the collection known today as the First Folio (F). The two texts are substantially different. F contains more than 150 lines not found in Q; Q has some 16 lines absent from F. And this is only the beginning: the two texts also exhibit more than 1,000 lexical variants. One obvious and important discrepancy is that Q omits Desdemona's "Willow Song." Another is that F omits virtually all instances of profanity and direct references to the deity, in keeping with the Parliamentary statute of 1606 forbidding blasphemy in stage plays. For example, at V.2.219, F gives Emilia the line "Oh heauen! oh heauenly Powres!" In Q she says, "O God! O heauenly God!" It appears, then, that the copy text for Q originated either before 1606 or else much later, when the decree was no longer strictly enforced. But even this is not certain.

The stumbling block in any effort to produce a modern text is that no one has been able to establish decisively the nature of the manuscripts used in the preparation of Q and F. Was Q based on an authorial manuscript? Was F? Was either printed from a theater promptbook? If so, was it F or Q? Might there have been more than one authorial manuscript, or a scribal and an authorial manuscript? Was F perhaps printed from Q, with reference to an authorial manuscript or prompt copy as a source for corrections? Many theories and diagrams and solutions have been proposed, and none has taken hold. Readers interested in pursuing the details and the implications of these problems are urged to consult Stanley Wells, Gary

Taylor, John Jowett, and William Montgomery, *William Shakespeare: A Textual Companion* (Oxford, 1987), E.A.J. Honigmann, *The Texts of "Othello" and Shakespearian Revision* (1996), the discussions of text in Honigmann's Arden edition (1997) and Norman Sanders's New Cambridge edition (1984), and Scott McMillin, "The *Othello* Quarto and the 'Foul-Paper' Hypothesis," *Shakespeare Quarterly,* 51 (2000): 67–85.

Most editors and textual scholars have agreed that F is the superior text, although Q presents many readings that seem preferable. Many previous editors, faced with the problem of two different words (F's "Judean" versus Q's "Indian" in Othello's final speech, for example) and lacking bibliographical evidence to guide them, often made their textual choice on grounds of taste. In other words, they usually chose F, the slightly longer version, as their copy text, but substituted words or phrases from Q on a case-by-case basis. The present edition uses F as the copy text and attempts to maintain a relatively strict policy on substitution or emendation. Thus, F's reading is retained if it seems at all possible – i.e., if it can be made to make sense, even if Q's alternative seems more appealing logically or artistically. The rationale for this practice is that each of the first two printings, F and Q, offers a version of the play that was satisfactory to someone – author or actor or editor or compiler – at about the time the play was written; that F, even with its weaknesses, is probably the better of these two alternatives; and that to conflate the two texts by selecting preferable readings gives the modern reader a version unknown in the early seventeenth century. In cases where F is clearly corrupt or unintelligible, the Q reading (if available) has been accepted. The one major exception to such strict fidelity to F involves censorship: on the grounds that the oaths and references to God were removed from F in response to censorship, I have restored these words with reference to Q. In some very rare cases, when the compositors of F seem to have made an error, the Q reading has been substituted. For example, at II.1.42, F's "Arriuancie" is probably a result of eye-skip from "expectancie" in the previous line; thus, Q's "arriuance" has been adopted. Stage directions from the folio are in italics only; those supplied (from Q and from theatrical necessity) to fill out the performance are placed within brackets.

The text produced here is imperfect, but so must be any text of this play. Below are listed all cases in which this edition departs from F (except for typographical errors). The adopted reading is printed in italics, followed by its source in parentheses: Q is the First Quarto, of 1622; Q2 is the Second Quarto, of 1630; names are those of previous editors. The rejected folio reading is given in roman.

The Names of the Actors (printed at the end of the text in F)
I.1 1 *Tush* (Q) omitted 4 *'Sblood* (Q) omitted 28 *other* (Q) others 32 *God* (Q) omitted 65 *full* (Q) fall; thick-lips (Q) Thicks-lips 85 *Zounds* (Q) omitted 107 *Zounds* (Q) omitted 121 *odd-even* (Malone) odde Euen 152 *pains* (Q) apines 180 *night* (Q) might
I.2 34 *duke* (Q) Dukes 68 *darlings* (Q) Deareling 84 *Where* (Q) Whether 87 *I* (Q) omitted
I.3 59 *ALL* (Q) Sen. 106 *DUKE* (Q) omitted 130 *battles* (Q) Battle; *fortunes* (Q) fortune 141 *and* (Q) omitted; *heads* (Q) head 143 *other* (Q) others 144 *anthropophagi* (Q) Antropophague 145 *Do grow* (Q) Grew 147 *thence* (Q) hence 155 *intentively* (Q) instinctiuely 201 *Into your favor* (Q) omitted 219 *ear* (Q) eares 230 *couch* (Pope) Coach 248 *did* (Q) omitted 263–64 *heat – the young affects / In me defunct –* (Capell) heat the yong affects / In my defunct, 270 *instruments* (Q) Instrument 299 *worldly* (Q) wordly; *matters* (Q) matter 326 *beam* (Theobald) braine 377 *a snipe* (Q) Snpe 380 *H'as* (Q) She ha's
II.1 33 *prays* (Q) praye 42 *arrivance* (Q) Arriuancie 65 *ingener* (Steevens) Ingeniuer 82 *And bring all Cyprus comfort!* (Q) omitted 88 *me* (Q) omitted 93 *(Within) A sail, a sail! [A shot.] But hark. A sail!* (Collier) But hearke, a Saile. / *Within.* A Saile, a Saile. 94 *their* (Q) this 213 *hither* (Q) thither 226 *again* (Q) a game 240 *has* (Q) he's 258–59 *mutualities* (Q) mutabilities 303 *rank* (Q) right
II.2 10 *Heaven* (Q) omitted
II.3 (New scene: Capell) 37 *unfortunate* (Q) infortunate 56 *to put* (Q) put to 60 *God* (Q) heauen 70 *God* (Q) Heauen 75 *Englishman* (Q) Englishmen 90 *Then* (Q) And; *auld* (Q) awl'd 92 *'Fore God* (Q) Why 96 *God's* (Q) heau'ns 105 *God* (Q) omitted 137 *(Within) Help! help!* (Q) omitted 138 *Zounds* (Q) omitted 146 *God's will* (Q2) Alas

150 *God's will, lieutenant, hold!* (Q) Fie, fie Lieutenant, 152 *Zounds* (Q) omitted 196 *Zounds, if I* (Q) If I once 207 *leagued* (Pope) league 250 *God* (Q) Heauen 278 *God* (Q) omitted 282 *Why,* (Q) Why? 320 *here* (Q) omitted 331 *were't* (Q) were 362 *hast* (Q) hath 365 *By the mass* (Q) Introth

III.1 21 *hear, mine* heare me, mine 25 *general's wife* (Q2) Generall 29 *CASSIO Do, good my friend* (Q) omitted

III.3 52 *Yes, faith* (Q) I sooth 63 *In faith* Infaith 74 *By'r Lady* (Q) Trust me 94 *you* (Q) he 106 *By heaven* (Q) Alas 112 *In* (Q) Of 139 *But some* (Q) Wherein 147 *oft* (Q) of 162 *By heaven* (Q) omitted 175 *God* (Q) Heauen 180 *once* (Q) omitted 202 *God* (Q) Heauen 204 *keep't* (Q) kept 215 *I' faith* (Q) Trust me 217 *my* (Q) your 248 *hold* (Q) omitted 259 *qualities* (Q) Quantities 273 *of* (Q) to 278 *O, then* (Q) omitted; *mocks* (Q) mock'd 285 *Faith* (Q) Why 311 *No, faith; she* (Q) No: but she 395 *supervisor* (Q) super-vision 424 *lay* (Rowe) laid 440 *that was* (Malone) it was 455 *feels* (Q2) keepes

III.4 54 *faith* (Q) indeed 75 *I' faith* (Q) Indeed 77 *God* (Q) Heauen 81 *Heaven* (Q) omitted 96 *I' faith* (Q) Insooth 97 *Zounds* (Q) Away 170 *I' faith* (Q) Indeed 181 *absence now* (Capell) Absence: now 186 *by my faith* (Q) in good troth

IV.1 32 *Faith* (Q) Why 36 *Zounds* (Q) omitted 52 *No, forbear* (Q) omitted 77 *unsuiting* (Q) resulting 101 *conster* (Q) conserue 103 *now* (Q) omitted 107 *power* (Q) dowre 110 *a* (Q) omitted 111 *i' faith* (Q) indeed 123 *Faith* (Q) Why 130 *beckons* (Q) becomes 160 *Faith* (Q) omitted 162 *Faith* (Q) Yes 212 *God* (Q) omitted 232 *By my troth* (Q) Trust me 242 *an* (Q) omitted

IV.2 30 *Nay* (Q) May 33 *But not the words* (Q) omitted 81 *Impudent strumpet!* (Q) omitted 141 *heaven* (Q) heauens 155 *them in* (Q2) them: or 167 *And he does chide with you* (Q) omitted 175 *daff'st* (Collier) dafts 182 *Faith* (Q) omitted

IV.3 22 *faith* (Q) Father 23 *thee* (Q) omitted 39 *sighing* (Q2) singing 74 *'Ud's pity* (Q) why 103 *God* (Q) Heauen

V.1 1 *bulk* (Q) Barke 35 *Forth* (Q) For 91 *O heaven* (Q) Yes, 'tis 105 *out* (Q) omitted

V.2 35 *so* (Q) omitted 57 *Then Lord* (Q) O Heauen 84 *DESDEMONA O Lord, Lord, Lord!* (Q) omitted 118 *O Lord* (Q) Alas 128 *heard* (Q) heare 219 *O God! O heavenly God!* (Q) Oh Heauen! oh heauenly Powres! 220 *Zounds* (Q) Come 241 *here* (Q) omitted 292 *damnèd* (Q) cursed

The Tragedy of Othello
the Moor of Venice

THE NAMES OF THE ACTORS*

OTHELLO, *the Moor [leader of the Venetian armed forces]*
BRABANTIO, *father to Desdemona*
CASSIO, *an honorable lieutenant*
IAGO, *a villain*
RODERIGO, *a gulled gentleman*
DUKE OF VENICE
SENATORS
MONTANO, *Governor of Cyprus*
GENTLEMEN OF CYPRUS
LODOVICO *and* GRATIANO, *two noble Venetians*
SAILORS
CLOWN
DESDEMONA, *wife to Othello*
EMILIA, *wife to Iago*
BIANCA, *a courtesan*
[MESSENGER, HERALD, OFFICERS, VENETIAN GENTLEMEN, MUSICIANS, ATTENDANTS]

[SCENE: *Venice and Cyprus*]
*

---

* This list, except for bracketed material, is printed at the end of the folio text.

The Tragedy
of Othello
the Moor of Venice

I.1 *Enter Roderigo and Iago.*

RODERIGO
  Tush, never tell me! I take it much unkindly
  That thou, Iago, who hast had my purse
  As if the strings were thine, shouldst know of this.

IAGO
  'Sblood, but you'll not hear me!   4
  If ever I did dream of such a matter,
  Abhor me.

RODERIGO
  Thou told'st me thou didst hold him in thy hate.

IAGO
  Despise me if I do not. Three great ones of the city,   8
  In personal suit to make me his lieutenant,
  Off-capped to him; and, by the faith of man,   10
  I know my price; I am worth no worse a place.
  But he, as loving his own pride and purposes,
  Evades them, with a bombast circumstance   13
  Horribly stuffed with epithets of war,
  Nonsuits my mediators; for, "Certes," says he,   15

I.1 A street in Venice   4 *'Sblood* (an oath; originally "by God's [i.e., Christ's]
blood")   8 *great ones* influential men   13 *bombast circumstance* pompous
evasion, roundabout excuses (*bombast* is cotton stuffing; see *stuffed*, l. 14)
15 *Nonsuits* denies

"I have already chose my officer."
And what was he?
18   Forsooth, a great arithmetician,
      One Michael Cassio, a Florentine
20   (A fellow almost damned in a fair wife)
      That never set a squadron in the field,
22   Nor the division of a battle knows
23   More than a spinster, unless the bookish theoric,
24   Wherein the tonguèd consuls can propose
      As masterly as he. Mere prattle without practice
      Is all his soldiership. But he, sir, had th' election;
      And I (of whom his eyes had seen the proof
      At Rhodes, at Cyprus, and on other grounds
29   Christened and heathen) must be beeled and calmed
30   By debitor and creditor. This countercaster,
      He, in good time, must his lieutenant be,
32   And I – God bless the mark! – his Moorship's ancient.
RODERIGO
      By heaven, I rather would have been his hangman.
IAGO
      Why, there's no remedy; 'tis the curse of service.
35   Preferment goes by letter and affection,
      And not by old gradation, where each second
      Stood heir to th' first. Now, sir, be judge yourself,
38   Whether I in any just term am affined
      To love the Moor.

---

18 *arithmetician* theorist, bean counter   20 *almost . . . wife* (a mystifying
reference, perhaps a result of error in textual transmission; although Cassio is
unmarried, the line links him with women early in the play)   22 *division of
a battle* arrangement of troops   23 *unless . . . theoric* except hypothetically
24 *tonguèd consuls* i.e., those who advise but don't actually fight   29 *beeled
and calmed* i.e., left behind; a nautical metaphor for frustration ("belee" = "to
place under the lee, or unfavorably to the wind")   30 *debitor and creditor*
bookkeeper; *countercaster* accountant   32 *God . . . mark* (an exclamation of
impatience); *ancient* ensign, standard-bearer (an officer inferior to lieutenant)   35–36 *Preferment . . . gradation* i.e., promotion now depends on
favoritism or whom you know, not on the old system of rising through the
ranks   38 *affined* bound

RODERIGO   I would not follow him then.

IAGO

   O, sir, content you;   40
   I follow him to serve my turn upon him.
   We cannot all be masters, nor all masters
   Cannot be truly followed. You shall mark
   Many a duteous and knee-crooking knave   44
   That, doting on his own obsequious bondage,   45
   Wears out his time, much like his master's ass,
   For nought but provender, and when he's old, cashiered.   47
   Whip me such honest knaves! Others there are   48
   Who, trimmed in forms and visages of duty,   49
   Keep yet their hearts attending on themselves,   50
   And, throwing but shows of service on their lords,
   Do well thrive by them, and when they have lined their
     coats,
   Do themselves homage. These fellows have some soul,   53
   And such a one do I profess myself. For, sir,
   It is as sure as you are Roderigo,
   Were I the Moor, I would not be Iago.
   In following him, I follow but myself.
   Heaven is my judge, not I for love and duty,
   But seeming so, for my peculiar end,   59
   For when my outward action doth demonstrate   60
   The native act and figure of my heart
   In complement extern, 'tis not long after
   But I will wear my heart upon my sleeve
   For daws to peck at. I am not what I am.   64

---

44 *knee-crooking* i.e., constantly bowing   45 *doting . . . bondage* i.e., loving
the role of the fawning servant   47 *provender* provisions, especially dry food
for animals; *cashiered* dismissed   48 *Whip me . . . knaves* (a common early
modern construction, the ethical dative, meaning "As for me, I say whip
such men")   49 *trimmed* dressed up; *visages* masks, appearances   50 *yet* still
53 *Do . . . homage* honor themselves by looking out for themselves   59 *peculiar end* private purpose   60–62 *my outward . . . complement extern* i.e.,
when my behavior corresponds to my real feelings   64 *daws* jackdaws
(proverbially foolish birds)

RODERIGO

65 What a full fortune does the thick-lips owe
66 If he can carry't thus!

IAGO   Call up her father,
Rouse him. Make after him, poison his delight,
Proclaim him in the streets. Incense her kinsmen,
And though he in a fertile climate dwell,
70 Plague him with flies. Though that his joy be joy,
71 Yet throw such chances of vexation on't
72 As it may lose some color.

RODERIGO
Here is her father's house. I'll call aloud.

IAGO
74 Do, with like timorous accent and dire yell
As when, by night and negligence, the fire
Is spied in populous cities.

RODERIGO
What, ho, Brabantio! Signor Brabantio, ho!

IAGO
Awake! What, ho, Brabantio! Thieves! thieves!
Look to your house, your daughter, and your bags!
80 Thieves! thieves!
    [Enter Brabantio] above.

BRABANTIO
What is the reason of this terrible summons?
What is the matter there?

RODERIGO
Signor, is all your family within?

IAGO
Are your doors locked?

BRABANTIO   Why, wherefore ask you this?

---

65 *the thick-lips* (a racist slur on Othello's African heritage); *owe* own 66 *carry't thus* bring it off (i.e., succeed) 71 *chances of vexation* possibilities for misery and embarrassment 72 *lose some color* i.e., his *joy* will fade 74 *timorous* frightening

IAGO

   Zounds, sir, you're robbed! For shame, put on your   85
     gown!
   Your heart is burst; you have lost half your soul.
   Even now, now, very now, an old black ram   87
   Is tupping your white ewe. Arise, arise!   88
   Awake the snorting citizens with the bell,   89
   Or else the devil will make a grandsire of you.   *90*
   Arise, I say!

BRABANTIO   What, have you lost your wits?

RODERIGO

   Most reverend signor, do you know my voice?

BRABANTIO

   Not I. What are you?

RODERIGO

   My name is Roderigo.

BRABANTIO   The worser welcome!

   I have charged thee not to haunt about my doors.
   In honest plainness thou hast heard me say
   My daughter is not for thee. And now, in madness,
   Being full of supper and distemp'ring draughts,   98
   Upon malicious knavery dost thou come
   To start my quiet.   100

RODERIGO

   Sir, sir, sir —

BRABANTIO   But thou must needs be sure

   My spirits and my place have in their power   102
   To make this bitter to thee.

RODERIGO   Patience, good sir.

BRABANTIO

   What tell'st thou me of robbing? This is Venice;

---

85 *Zounds* (an oath; originally "by God's [i.e., Christ's] wounds") 87 *very now* at this very moment 88 *tupping* copulating with (used specifically of rams) 89 *snorting* snoring 98 *distemp'ring draughts* intoxicating drinks 100 *start my quiet* disturb my peace 102 *spirits* emotions (i.e., anger)

105   My house is not a grange.
        RODERIGO   Most grave Brabantio,
        In simple and pure soul I come to you.
        IAGO   Zounds, sir, you are one of those that will not
        serve God if the devil bid you. Because we come to do
        you service, and you think we are ruffians, you'll have
110   your daughter covered with a Barbary horse; you'll have
111   your nephews neigh to you; you'll have coursers for
112   cousins, and jennets for germans.
        BRABANTIO
        What profane wretch art thou?
        IAGO   I am one, sir, that comes to tell you your daughter
115   and the Moor are making the beast with two backs.
        BRABANTIO
        Thou art a villain.
        IAGO   You are – a senator.
        BRABANTIO
        This thou shalt answer. I know thee, Roderigo.
        RODERIGO
        Sir, I will answer anything. But I beseech you,
        If't be your pleasure and most wise consent,
120   As partly I find it is, that your fair daughter,
121   At this odd-even and dull watch o' th' night,
        Transported, with no worse nor better guard
        But with a knave of common hire, a gondolier,
        To the gross clasps of a lascivious Moor –
125   If this be known to you, and your allowance,
        We then have done you bold and saucy wrongs.
        But if you know not this, my manners tell me,
        We have your wrong rebuke. Do not believe

---

105 *grange* farmhouse   110 *covered . . . horse* (another figure for bestial cop-
ulation; Barbary was the home of Berbers, or Moors)   111 *nephews* (kinsmen generally; here grandsons)   111–12 *coursers for cousins* racehorses for
relatives   112 *jennets for germans* small Spanish horses for near kinsmen
115 *beast with two backs* (a visual symbol of sexual intercourse)   121 *odd-
even and dull watch* i.e., in-between and sleepy hour, perhaps midnight (between evening and morning)   125 *allowance* approval

That, from the sense of all civility,   129
I thus would play and trifle with your reverence.   *130*
Your daughter, if you have not given her leave,
I say again, hath made a gross revolt,
Tying her duty, beauty, wit, and fortunes
In an extravagant and wheeling stranger   134
Of here and everywhere. Straight satisfy yourself.   135
If she be in her chamber, or your house,
Let loose on me the justice of the state
For thus deluding you.   138
BRABANTIO   Strike on the tinder, ho!
Give me a taper! Call up all my people!
This accident is not unlike my dream.   140
Belief of it oppresses me already.
Light, I say! light!   *Exit [above].*
IAGO   Farewell, for I must leave you.
It seems not meet, nor wholesome to my place,
To be producted – as, if I stay, I shall –   144
Against the Moor. For I do know the state,
However this may gall him with some check,   146
Cannot with safety cast him; for he's embarked   147
With such loud reason to the Cyprus wars,
Which even now stands in act, that for their souls   149
Another of his fathom they have none   150
To lead their business; in which regard,
Though I do hate him as I do hell pains,
Yet, for necessity of present life,
I must show out a flag and sign of love,
Which is indeed but sign. That you shall surely find
   him,
Lead to the Sagittary the raisèd search;   156

---

129 *from the sense of* against   134 *extravagant and wheeling* i.e., far from
home and rootless, roving   135 *Straight* straightaway, immediately   138
tinder tinderbox (for a light)   140 *accident* occurrence   144 *producted* produced (i.e., called as a witness)   146 *check* reprimand   147 *cast* dismiss
149 *stands in act* is imminent; *for their souls* i.e., to save their souls   150
fathom deep capacity (i.e., talent)   156 *the Sagittary* (an inn)

157   And there will I be with him. So farewell.   *Exit.*
        Enter Brabantio [below, in his nightgown], with
        Servants and Torches.
        BRABANTIO
        It is too true an evil. Gone she is,
159   And what's to come of my despisèd time
160   Is nought but bitterness. Now, Roderigo,
        Where didst thou see her? – O unhappy girl! –
        With the Moor, say'st thou? – Who would be a father?–
        How didst thou know 'twas she? – O, she deceives me
        Past thought! – What said she to you? – Get more ta-
        pers!
        Raise all my kindred! – Are they married, think you?
        RODERIGO
        Truly I think they are.
        BRABANTIO
        O heaven! How got she out? O treason of the blood!
        Fathers, from hence trust not your daughters' minds
        By what you see them act. Is there not charms
170   By which the property of youth and maidhood
        May be abused? Have you not read, Roderigo,
        Of some such thing?
        RODERIGO   Yes, sir, I have indeed.
        BRABANTIO
        Call up my brother. – O, would you had had her! –
        Some one way, some another. – Do you know
        Where we may apprehend her and the Moor?
        RODERIGO
        I think I can discover him, if you please
        To get good guard and go along with me.
        BRABANTIO
        Pray you lead on. At every house I'll call;
        I may command at most. – Get weapons, ho!

        ───────
        157 s.d. *nightgown* dressing gown; *Torches* torchbearers **159** *despisèd time*
        unfortunate life **170** *property* natural behavior

And raise some special officers of night. –   180
On, good Roderigo; I will deserve your pains. *Exeunt.* 181

                              *

∾ **I.2** *Enter Othello, Iago, Attendants, with Torches.*

IAGO
  Though in the trade of war I have slain men,
  Yet do I hold it very stuff o' th' conscience   2
  To do no contrived murder. I lack iniquity
  Sometime to do me service. Nine or ten times
  I had thought t' have yerked him here under the ribs.   5
OTHELLO
  'Tis better as it is.   6
IAGO   Nay, but he prated,
  And spoke such scurvy and provoking terms
  Against your honor
  That with the little godliness I have
  I did full hard forbear him. But I pray you, sir,   10
  Are you fast married? Be assured of this,   11
  That the magnifico is much beloved,   12
  And hath in his effect a voice potential   13
  As double as the duke's. He will divorce you,
  Or put upon you what restraint or grievance
  The law, with all his might to enforce it on,
  Will give him cable.   17
OTHELLO   Let him do his spite.
  My services which I have done the signory   18

---

180 *special . . . night* (a famous Venetian nocturnal patrol) **181** *deserve*
repay
  I.2 The street in front of the Sagittary **2** *very stuff* the essence **5** *yerked*
struck or (as with a horse) kicked *under the ribs* **6** *prated* babbled **10** *did
full hard forbear* i.e., barely tolerated **11** *fast* securely **12** *magnifico* aristocrat (i.e., Brabantio) **13–14** *a voice . . . duke's* i.e., an influence twice as
great as the duke's **17** *give him cable* i.e., allow him freedom **18** *signory*
Venetian political establishment

19   Shall out-tongue his complaints. 'Tis yet to know –
20   Which, when I know that boasting is an honor,
21   I shall promulgate – I fetch my life and being
22   From men of royal siege, and my demerits
23   May speak unbonneted to as proud a fortune
      As this that I have reached. For know, Iago,
      But that I love the gentle Desdemona,
26   I would not my unhousèd free condition
      Put into circumscription and confine
      For the sea's worth. But look, what lights come yond?
      Enter Cassio [and Officers] with Torches.
IAGO
29   Those are the raisèd father and his friends.
30   You were best go in.
OTHELLO   Not I; I must be found.
31   My parts, my title, and my perfect soul
32   Shall manifest me rightly. Is it they?
IAGO
33   By Janus, I think no.
OTHELLO
      The servants of the duke? And my lieutenant?
      The goodness of the night upon you, friends!
      What is the news?
CASSIO   The duke does greet you, general,
      And he requires your haste-posthaste appearance
      Even on the instant.
OTHELLO   What is the matter, think you?
CASSIO
39   Something from Cyprus, as I may divine.

---

19 *yet to know* still not generally known 21 *promulgate* broadcast, make known 22 *siege* seat (i.e., rank or status); *demerits* merits, deserts (obsolete form) 23–24 *May speak . . . have reached* i.e., can without boasting claim worldly success equal to that of Desdemona's family (*this that I have reached*) 26–27 *my unhousèd . . . and confine* i.e., trade the outdoors for domesticity, my independence for limits 29 *raisèd* roused, alarmed 31 *parts* abilities; *perfect soul* clear conscience 32 *manifest me* i.e., make my case 33 *Janus* the two-faced Roman god 39 *as I may divine* i.e., I suppose

It is a business of some heat. The galleys   40
Have sent a dozen sequent messengers   41
This very night at one another's heels,
And many of the consuls, raised and met,
Are at the duke's already. You have been hotly called for;
When being not at your lodging to be found,
The Senate hath sent about three several quests   46
To search you out.
OTHELLO   'Tis well I am found by you.
I will but spend a word here in the house,
And go with you.   *[Exit.]*
CASSIO   Ancient, what makes he here?
IAGO
Faith, he tonight hath boarded a land carrack.   50
If it prove lawful prize, he's made forever.
CASSIO
I do not understand.
IAGO   He's married.
CASSIO   To who?
    [Enter Othello.]
IAGO
Marry, to – Come, captain, will you go?   53
OTHELLO   Have with you.
CASSIO
Here comes another troop to seek for you.
    Enter Brabantio, Roderigo, with Officers and Torches.
IAGO
It is Brabantio. General, be advised.
He comes to bad intent.
OTHELLO   Holla! stand there!
RODERIGO
Signor, it is the Moor.
BRABANTIO   Down with him, thief!
    [They draw on both sides.]

---

40 *heat* intensity or urgency **41** *sequent* consecutive **46** *sent about* sent
out; *several* separate **50** *Faith* by my faith, in faith (a mild oath); *carrack*
treasure ship **53** *Marry* (a mild form of the oath "By the Virgin Mary")

IAGO
58   You, Roderigo! Come, sir, I am for you.
OTHELLO
59   Keep up your bright swords, for the dew will rust them.
60   Good signor, you shall more command with years
     Than with your weapons.
BRABANTIO
     O thou foul thief, where hast thou stowed my daughter?
     Damned as thou art, thou hast enchanted her!
     For I'll refer me to all things of sense,
     If she in chains of magic were not bound,
     Whether a maid so tender, fair, and happy,
     So opposite to marriage that she shunned
     The wealthy curlèd darlings of our nation,
69   Would ever have, t' incur a general mock,
70   Run from her guardage to the sooty bosom
     Of such a thing as thou – to fear, not to delight.
72   Judge me the world if 'tis not gross in sense
     That thou hast practiced on her with foul charms,
     Abused her delicate youth with drugs or minerals
75   That weakens motion. I'll have't disputed on;
     'Tis probable, and palpable to thinking.
77   I therefore apprehend and do attach thee
     For an abuser of the world, a practicer
     Of arts inhibited and out of warrant.
80   Lay hold upon him. If he do resist,
     Subdue him at his peril.
OTHELLO   Hold your hands,
     Both you of my inclining and the rest.
     Were it my cue to fight, I should have known it
     Without a prompter. Where will you that I go

---

58 *am for you* challenge you   59 *Keep up* i.e., sheathe, put away   69 *a general mock* universal laughter   72 *gross in sense* obvious   75 *motion* perception; *disputed on* brought to law   77 *attach* arrest

    To answer this your charge?
BRABANTIO   To prison, till fit time
    Of law and course of direct session   86
    Call thee to answer.
OTHELLO   What if I do obey?
    How may the duke be therewith satisfied,
    Whose messengers are here about my side
    Upon some present business of the state   90
    To bring me to him?
OFFICER   'Tis true, most worthy signor.
    The duke's in council, and your noble self
    I am sure is sent for.
BRABANTIO   How? The duke in council?
    In this time of the night? Bring him away.
    Mine's not an idle cause. The duke himself,   95
    Or any of my brothers of the state,
    Cannot but feel this wrong as 'twere their own;
    For if such actions may have passage free,
    Bondslaves and pagans shall our statesmen be. *Exeunt.*

*

∾ **I.3** *Enter Duke, Senators, and Officers [with lights].*

DUKE
    There's no composition in this news   1
    That gives them credit.
FIRST SENATOR   Indeed they are disproportioned.
    My letters say a hundred and seven galleys.
DUKE
    And mine a hundred forty.
SECOND SENATOR   And mine two hundred.
    But though they jump not on a just account –   5

---

86 *direct session* regular trial   95 *idle* inconsequential
    I.3 The Venetian Senate Chamber   1 *composition* consistency; *news*
newly received information   5 *jump* agree; *just account* precise estimate

6   As in these cases where the aim reports
       'Tis oft with difference – yet do they all confirm
       A Turkish fleet, and bearing up to Cyprus.
   DUKE
       Nay, it is possible enough to judgment.
10   I do not so secure me in the error
       But the main article I do approve
       In fearful sense.
   SAILOR *Within*
                          What, ho! what, ho! what, ho!
       Enter Sailor.
   OFFICER
       A messenger from the galleys.
   DUKE   Now, what's the business?
   SAILOR
14   The Turkish preparation makes for Rhodes.
       So was I bid report here to the state
       By Signor Angelo.
   DUKE
       How say you by this change?
   FIRST SENATOR   This cannot be
18   By no assay of reason. 'Tis a pageant
19   To keep us in false gaze. When we consider
20   Th' importancy of Cyprus to the Turk,
       And let ourselves again but understand
       That, as it more concerns the Turk than Rhodes,
23   So may he with more facile question bear it,
24   For that it stands not in such warlike brace,
       But altogether lacks th' abilities
       That Rhodes is dressed in – if we make thought of this,
       We must not think the Turk is so unskillful
28   To leave that latest which concerns him first,

---

6 *aim* guess 10–12 *I do not . . . sense* the discrepancies of the reports aren't
enough to cancel the frightening substance (*main article*) of them 14 *preparation* forces, assembled fleet 18 *assay* test, effort; *pageant* sideshow 19 *in
false gaze* looking the wrong way 23 *with . . . it* capture it more easily 24
brace state of defense 28 *latest* last

Neglecting an attempt of ease and gain
To wake and wage a danger profitless.   30

DUKE

Nay, in all confidence, he's not for Rhodes.

OFFICER

Here is more news.

Enter a Messenger.

MESSENGER

The Ottomites, reverend and gracious,   33
Steering with due course toward the isle of Rhodes,   34
Have there injointed them with an after fleet.   35

FIRST SENATOR

Ay, so I thought. How many, as you guess?

MESSENGER

Of thirty sail; and now they do restem   37
Their backward course, bearing with frank appearance   38
Their purposes toward Cyprus. Signor Montano,
Your trusty and most valiant servitor,   40
With his free duty recommends you thus   41
And prays you to believe him.

DUKE

'Tis certain then for Cyprus.
Marcus Luccicos, is not he in town?

FIRST SENATOR

He's now in Florence.

DUKE

Write from us to him post-posthaste. Dispatch!

FIRST SENATOR

Here comes Brabantio and the valiant Moor.

Enter Brabantio, Othello, Cassio, Iago, Roderigo, and
Officers.

---

30 *wake and wage* rouse and risk   **33** *Ottomites* Turkish fleet (Turks and Ottomites seem to have been identified in the Elizabethan mind); *reverend and
gracious* (honorific term of address to the assembly)   **34** *due* direct   **35** *injointed* combined (themselves); *after fleet* a subordinate or secondary navy
37 *restem* steer again   **38** *with frank appearance* openly, without deceit   **41**
free duty unlimited loyalty; *recommends* informs

DUKE

48 Valiant Othello, we must straight employ you
Against the general enemy Ottoman.
[To Brabantio]

50 I did not see you. Welcome, gentle signor.
We lacked your counsel and your help tonight.

BRABANTIO

So did I yours. Good your grace, pardon me.

53 Neither my place, nor aught I heard of business,
Hath raised me from my bed; nor doth the general care
Take hold on me; for my particular grief

56 Is of so floodgate and o'erbearing nature

57 That it engluts and swallows other sorrows,
And it is still itself.

DUKE   Why, what's the matter?

BRABANTIO

My daughter! O, my daughter!

ALL   Dead?

BRABANTIO   Ay, to me.

60 She is abused, stol'n from me, and corrupted

61 By spells and medicines bought of mountebanks;
For nature so prepost'rously to err,

63 Being not deficient, blind, or lame of sense,
Sans witchcraft could not.

DUKE

Whoe'er he be that in this foul proceeding
Hath thus beguiled your daughter of herself,

67 And you of her, the bloody book of law
You shall yourself read in the bitter letter

69 After your own sense; yea, though our proper son

70 Stood in your action.

---

48 *straight* straightaway, immediately   53 *place* position (as senator)   56 *of
so floodgate* so torrential   57 *engluts* gulps down   60 *abused* deceived   61
mountebanks quacks or scam artists (for which Venice was notorious)   63
deficient feebleminded   67–69 *bloody . . . sense* i.e., you may interpret the
law in the strictest sense that suits you   69 *our proper* my own   70 *Stood in
your action* were the object of your charges

BRABANTIO   Humbly I thank your grace.
  Here is the man – this Moor, whom now, it seems,
  Your special mandate for the state affairs
  Hath hither brought.
ALL   We are very sorry for't.
DUKE   *[To Othello]*
  What, in your own part, can you say to this?
BRABANTIO
  Nothing, but this is so.
OTHELLO
  Most potent, grave, and reverend signors,
  My very noble and approved good masters,   77
  That I have ta'en away this old man's daughter,
  It is most true; true I have married her.
  The very head and front of my offending   80
  Hath this extent, no more. Rude am I in my speech,   81
  And little blessed with the soft phrase of peace;
  For since these arms of mine had seven years' pith   83
  Till now some nine moons wasted, they have used   84
  Their dearest action in the tented field;   85
  And little of this great world can I speak
  More than pertains to feats of broils and battle;   87
  And therefore little shall I grace my cause
  In speaking for myself. Yet, by your gracious patience,
  I will a round unvarnished tale deliver   90
  Of my whole course of love – what drugs, what
    charms,
  What conjuration, and what mighty magic
  (For such proceeding I am charged withal)
  I won his daughter.
BRABANTIO   A maiden never bold;
  Of spirit so still and quiet that her motion   95

---

77 *approved* tested by experience   81 *Rude* unskilled, unpolished   83 *pith* strength   84 *wasted* gone by   85 *dearest* most valuable   87 *broils* strife, hurly-burly   90 *round* plain   95–96 *her motion / Blushed* her own feelings caused her to blush

Blushed at herself; and she – in spite of nature,
97   Of years, of country, credit, everything –
To fall in love with what she feared to look on!
It is a judgment maimed and most imperfect
100   That will confess perfection so could err
101   Against all rules of nature, and must be driven
To find out practices of cunning hell
103   Why this should be. I therefore vouch again
104   That with some mixtures pow'rful o'er the blood,
105   Or with some dram, conjured to this effect,
He wrought upon her.
DUKE   To vouch this is no proof,
107   Without more wider and more overt test
108   Than these thin habits and poor likelihoods
Of modern seeming do prefer against him.
SENATOR
110   But, Othello, speak.
111   Did you by indirect and forcèd courses
Subdue and poison this young maid's affections?
113   Or came it by request, and such fair question
As soul to soul affordeth?
OTHELLO   I do beseech you,
Send for the lady to the Sagittary
And let her speak of me before her father.
117   If you do find me foul in her report,
The trust, the office, I do hold of you
Not only take away, but let your sentence
120   Even fall upon my life.
DUKE   Fetch Desdemona hither.

---

97 *credit* reputation   101–2 *must be driven . . . hell* i.e., the reasonable mind
must seek diabolical plots   103 *vouch* claim   104 *blood* passions, sexual appetite   105 *dram* small portion; *conjured* bewitched, magically produced
(accent on second syllable)   107 *more wider . . . overt* more thorough and
manifest (i.e., convincing)   108–9 *these thin . . . seeming* i.e., these flimsy
signs and conclusions drawn from ordinary appearances   111 *forcèd* (1) unnatural, (2) coercive   113 *question* talk, conversation   117 *foul* ugly (also
"dark," perhaps Othello's ironic reference to his own color)

OTHELLO
　Ancient, conduct them; you best know the place.
　　　　　　　[Exit two or three Officers with Iago.]
　And till she come, as truly as to heaven
　I do confess the vices of my blood,
　So justly to your grave ears I'll present
　How I did thrive in this fair lady's love,
　And she in mine.

DUKE
　Say it, Othello.

OTHELLO
　Her father loved me, oft invited me,
　Still questioned me the story of my life   129
　From year to year – the battles, sieges, fortunes   *130*
　That I have passed.
　I ran it through, even from my boyish days
　To th' very moment that he bade me tell it.
　Wherein I spoke of most disastrous chances,   134
　Of moving accidents by flood and field;   135
　Of hairbreadth scapes i' th' imminent deadly breach;   136
　Of being taken by the insolent foe   137
　And sold to slavery. Of my redemption thence
　And portance in my traveler's history,   139
　Wherein of anters vast and deserts idle,   140
　Rough quarries, rocks, and hills whose heads touch
　　heaven,
　It was my hint to speak – such was my process;   142
　And of the cannibals that each other eat,
　The anthropophagi, and men whose heads   144
　Do grow beneath their shoulders. These things to hear
　Would Desdemona seriously incline;

---

129 *Still* constantly   134 *disastrous* unlucky (Latin "ill-starred")   135 *accidents by flood and field* occurrences on sea and land   136 *in . . . deadly breach* gap in a defense inviting immediate disaster   137 *insolent* (1) arrogant, (2) insulting   139 *portance* behavior, bearing; *traveler's history* (a minor subgenre of writing c. 1600, often containing tall tales)   140 *anters* caves   142 *hint* occasion, opportunity; *process* drift   144 *anthropophagi* man-eaters

But still the house affairs would draw her thence,
Which ever as she could with haste dispatch,
She'd come again, and with a greedy ear
150 Devour up my discourse. Which I observing,
151 Took once a pliant hour, and found good means
To draw from her a prayer of earnest heart
153 That I would all my pilgrimage dilate,
154 Whereof by parcels she had something heard,
155 But not intentively. I did consent,
And often did beguile her of her tears
When I did speak of some distressful stroke
That my youth suffered. My story being done,
She gave me for my pains a world of kisses.
160 She swore in faith 'twas strange, 'twas passing strange;
'Twas pitiful, 'twas wondrous pitiful.
She wished she had not heard it, yet she wished
That heaven had made her such a man. She thanked
          me,
And bade me, if I had a friend that loved her,
I should but teach him how to tell my story,
166 And that would woo her. Upon this hint I spake.
She loved me for the dangers I had passed,
And I loved her that she did pity them.
This only is the witchcraft I have used.
170 Here comes the lady. Let her witness it.
          Enter Desdemona, Iago, Attendants.
DUKE
     I think this tale would win my daughter too.
     Good Brabantio,
     Take up this mangled matter at the best.
     Men do their broken weapons rather use
     Than their bare hands.

---

151 *pliant* convenient   153 *dilate* expand upon   154 *by parcels* in bits and pieces   155 *intentively* i.e., with her full attention   166 *hint* opportunity (as at l. 142)

BRABANTIO   I pray you hear her speak.
  If she confess that she was half the wooer,
  Destruction on my head if my bad blame
  Light on the man! Come hither, gentle mistress.
  Do you perceive in all this noble company
  Where most you owe obedience?   *180*
DESDEMONA   My noble father,
  I do perceive here a divided duty.
  To you I am bound for life and education.   182
  My life and education both do learn me
  How to respect you: you are the lord of duty;
  I am hitherto your daughter. But here's my husband;
  And so much duty as my mother showed
  To you, preferring you before her father,
  So much I challenge that I may profess   188
  Due to the Moor my lord.
BRABANTIO   God be with you! I have done.
  Please it your grace, on to the state affairs.   *190*
  I had rather to adopt a child than get it.   191
  Come hither, Moor.
  I here do give thee that with all my heart
  Which, but thou hast already, with all my heart   194
  I would keep from thee. For your sake, jewel,   195
  I am glad at soul I have no other child,
  For thy escape would teach me tyranny,   197
  To hang clogs on them. I have done, my lord.   198
DUKE
  Let me speak like yourself and lay a sentence   199
  Which, as a grece or step, may help these lovers   200

---

182 *education* rearing 188 *challenge* assert the right 191 *get* beget 194
but thou hast already if you didn't have it already 195 *For your sake* thanks to
you 197 *escape* transgression, escapade 198 *clogs* weights (of the kind at-
tached to prisoners; in the seventeenth century they were made of blocks of
wood) 199 *like yourself* as you should; *sentence* brief sermon or maxim (i.e.,
the following rhymed couplets of advice) 200 *grece* stairstep

Into your favor.
202   When remedies are past, the griefs are ended
        By seeing the worst, which late on hopes depended.
        To mourn a mischief that is past and gone
        Is the next way to draw new mischief on.
206   What cannot be preserved when fortune takes,
        Patience her injury a mock'ry makes.
        The robbed that smiles steals something from the thief;
209   He robs himself that spends a bootless grief.

BRABANTIO

210   So let the Turk of Cyprus us beguile:
        We lose it not so long as we can smile.
212   He bears the sentence well that nothing bears
        But the free comfort which from thence he hears;
        But he bears both the sentence and the sorrow
        That to pay grief must of poor patience borrow.
        These sentences, to sugar, or to gall,
        Being strong on both sides, are equivocal.
        But words are words. I never yet did hear
219   That the bruised heart was pierced through the ear.
220   I humbly beseech you proceed to th' affairs of state.

DUKE   The Turk with a most mighty preparation makes
222   for Cyprus. Othello, the fortitude of the place is best
223   known to you; and though we have there a substitute of
224   most allowed sufficiency, yet opinion, a more sovereign

---

202-3 *When remedies . . . depended* i.e., disappointment is best mended by
facing the unhappy outcome that you feared 206-7 *What cannot . . .
mock'ry makes* to show *patience* when one is unfortunate is to ridicule and
thus show superiority to *fortune* 209 *spends a bootless grief* indulges in
worthless lamentation 210 *So* in that case; *of Cyprus us beguile* cheat us out
of possession of Cyprus 212-15 *He bears . . . borrow* i.e., he who can simply take the advice and forget the injury is lucky, but he who is still sorrow-
ful (who has to borrow from *patience* to *pay* a debt to *grief*) has to put up
with the lecture and the misery 219 *pierced* (some editors emend to
"pieced" – i.e., "mended") 222 *fortitude* defensive strength, fortification
223 *substitute* governor or deputy (another instance of replacement in the
play) 224 *allowed* acknowledged; *opinion* reputation 224-25 *more sovereign mistress of effects* better predictor of outcomes

mistress of effects, throws a more safer voice on you.
You must therefore be content to slubber the gloss   226
of your new fortunes with this more stubborn and   227
boist'rous expedition.

OTHELLO
The tyrant custom, most grave senators,
Hath made the flinty and steel couch of war   *230*
My thrice-driven bed of down. I do agnize   231
A natural and prompt alacrity
I find in hardness; and do undertake
This present wars against the Ottomites.
Most humbly, therefore, bending to your state,   235
I crave fit disposition for my wife,   236
Due reference of place, and exhibition,   237
With such accommodation and besort   238
As levels with her breeding.   239

DUKE
Why, at her father's.   *240*

BRABANTIO   I will not have it so.

OTHELLO
Nor I.

DESDEMONA   Nor would I there reside,
To put my father in impatient thoughts
By being in his eye. Most gracious duke,
To my unfolding lend your prosperous ear,   244
And let me find a charter in your voice,   245
T' assist my simpleness.   246

DUKE
What would you, Desdemona?

---

226 *slubber* stain or darken   227 *stubborn* untamable   231 *thrice-driven bed of down* feather bed winnowed three times to make it supersoft   231–33 *agnize . . . hardness* i.e., recognize in myself a taste (*alacrity*) for hardship or challenge   235 *bending to your state* i.e., bowing to your position   236 *fit disposition* appropriate arrangements   237 *reference of place* assignment of residence; *exhibition* allowance   238 *besort* companions   239 *levels with* matches   244 *prosperous* favorable   245 *a charter* license, authority   246 *simpleness* inexperience

DESDEMONA
That I did love the Moor to live with him,
249 My downright violence, and storm of fortunes,
250 May trumpet to the world. My heart's subdued
251 Even to the very quality of my lord.
252 I saw Othello's visage in his mind,
253 And to his honors and his valiant parts
Did I my soul and fortunes consecrate.
So that, dear lords, if I be left behind,
A moth of peace, and he go to the war,
257 The rites for why I love him are bereft me,
And I a heavy interim shall support
259 By his dear absence. Let me go with him.
OTHELLO
260 Let her have your voice.
Vouch with me, heaven, I therefore beg it not
To please the palate of my appetite,
263 Nor to comply with heat – the young affects
In me defunct – and proper satisfaction;
But to be free and bounteous to her mind.
And heaven defend your good souls that you think
I will your serious and great business scant
268 When she is with me. No, when light-winged toys
269 Of feathered Cupid seel with wanton dullness
270 My speculative and officed instruments,
271 That my disports corrupt and taint my business,
Let housewives make a skillet of my helm,
273 And all indign and base adversities

---

249 *downright violence* obvious unconventionality (*violence* against propriety); *storm of fortunes* i.e., the tempestuous results of that unconventionality
251 *quality* essential nature   252 *I saw . . . his mind* i.e., I looked within Othello, replacing his dark face (*visage*) with his *mind*   253 *parts* talents, gifts   257 *rites* ceremonies or perhaps also "rights," privileges of marriage
259 *dear* costly, grievous   263 *comply with heat* follow the dictates of passion; *young affects* youthful desires   268–69 *light-winged toys . . . Cupid* trivial sports of love   269–70 *seel . . . instruments* i.e., blind my vision (*speculative and officed instruments*) with the low desires of the body   271 *That* such that; *disports* i.e., sexual pleasures   273 *indign* shameful

Make head against my estimation!   274
DUKE
  Be it as you shall privately determine,
  Either for her stay or going. Th' affair cries haste,
  And speed must answer it.
SENATOR
  You must away tonight.
OTHELLO   With all my heart.
DUKE
  At nine i' th' morning here we'll meet again.
  Othello, leave some officer behind,   280
  And he shall our commission bring to you,
  And such things else of quality and respect
  As doth import you.   283
OTHELLO   So please your grace, my ancient;
  A man he is of honesty and trust.
  To his conveyance I assign my wife,   285
  With what else needful your good grace shall think
  To be sent after me.
DUKE   Let it be so.
  Good night to every one.
      [To Brabantio]   And, noble signor,
  If virtue no delighted beauty lack,   289
  Your son-in-law is far more fair than black.   290
SENATOR
  Adieu, brave Moor. Use Desdemona well.
BRABANTIO
  Look to her, Moor, if thou hast eyes to see:
  She has deceived her father, and may thee.
                    Exit [Duke, with Senators, Officers, etc.].
OTHELLO
  My life upon her faith! – Honest Iago,   294
  My Desdemona must I leave to thee.

---

274 *Make head* mount an attack; *estimation* reputation 283 *import* concern
285 *conveyance* escorting 289 *If virtue . . . lack* if worthiness (*virtue*) has the
power to be delightful (*delighted*) 294 *faith* fidelity, faithfulness

I prithee let thy wife attend on her,
297   And bring them after in the best advantage.
Come, Desdemona. I have but an hour
299   Of love, of worldly matters and direction,
300   To spend with thee. We must obey the time.

Exit [Othello with Desdemona].

RODERIGO Iago –
IAGO What say'st thou, noble heart?
RODERIGO What will I do, think'st thou?
IAGO Why, go to bed and sleep.
305 RODERIGO I will incontinently drown myself.
IAGO If thou dost, I shall never love thee after. Why,
thou silly gentleman?
RODERIGO It is silliness to live when to live is torment,
309   and then have we a prescription to die when death is
310   our physician.
IAGO O villainous! I have looked upon the world for
four times seven years, and since I could distinguish betwixt a benefit and an injury, I never found man that
knew how to love himself. Ere I would say I would
315   drown myself for the love of a guinea hen, I would
change my humanity with a baboon.
RODERIGO What should I do? I confess it is my shame
318   to be so fond, but it is not in my virtue to amend it.
IAGO Virtue? a fig! 'Tis in ourselves that we are thus or
320   thus. Our bodies are our gardens, to the which our
321   wills are gardeners; so that if we will plant nettles or
sow lettuce, set hyssop and weed up thyme, supply
323   it with one gender of herbs or distract it with many –

---

297 *in the best advantage* at the most opportune time 299 *direction* oversee-
ing business 305 *incontinently* immediately 309–10 *have . . . physician*
ancient custom (*prescription*) leads us to kill ourselves if doing so will cure
our ills 315 *guinea hen* bird (figuratively, slang term for a woman; cf.
"chick") 318 *virtue* power, ability 321 *wills* desires (but the term is sexually loaded: in the period its specific sense of "erotic desire" was supplemented with numerous connotations, from "penis" to "vagina") 323 *gender*
kind (cf. "genre"); *distract* divide

either to have it sterile with idleness or manured with   324
industry – why, the power and corrigible authority of   325
this lies in our wills. If the beam of our lives had not
one scale of reason to poise another of sensuality, the   327
blood and baseness of our natures would conduct us to   328
most prepost'rous conclusions. But we have reason to
cool our raging motions, our carnal stings or unbitted   330
lusts; whereof I take this that you call love to be a sect   331
or scion.

RODERIGO   It cannot be.

IAGO   It is merely a lust of the blood and a permission of   334
the will. Come, be a man! Drown thyself? Drown cats
and blind puppies! I have professed me thy friend, and
I confess me knit to thy deserving with cables of per-   337
durable toughness. I could never better stead thee than   338
now. Put money in thy purse. Follow thou the wars; de-   339
feat thy favor with an usurped beard. I say, put money   *340*
in thy purse. It cannot be long that Desdemona should
continue her love to the Moor – put money in thy
purse – nor he his to her. It was a violent commence-
ment in her, and thou shalt see an answerable seques-   344
tration – put but money in thy purse. These Moors are
changeable in their wills – fill thy purse with money.
The food that to him now is as luscious as locusts shall   347
be to him shortly as bitter as coloquintida. She must   348
change for youth: when she is sated with his body, she
will find the errors of her choice. Therefore put money   *350*
in thy purse. If thou wilt needs damn thyself, do it a

324–25 *sterile . . . industry* either unproductive or richly cultivated   325
corrigible authority power to correct   327 *poise* counterbalance   328 *blood and baseness* bestial instincts   330 *motions* impulses; *unbitted* uncontrolled, unbridled   331–32 *a sect or scion* an offshoot or a cutting   334 *merely* completely (i.e., nothing more than)   337–38 *perdurable* unbreakable   338 *stead* help   339–40 *defeat thy favor* undo your facial appearance (i.e., disguise yourself by putting on *an usurped* [counterfeit] *beard*)   344–45 *answerable sequestration* equivalent separation   347 *locusts* carobs, known for their sweet juice   348 *coloquintida* medicine made from the colocynth, a bitter apple

352 more delicate way than drowning. Make all the money
353 thou canst. If sanctimony and a frail vow betwixt an
354 erring barbarian and supersubtle Venetian be not too
hard for my wits and all the tribe of hell, thou shalt
356 enjoy her. Therefore make money. A pox of drowning
357 thyself! – it is clean out of the way. Seek thou rather to
be hanged in compassing thy joy than to be drowned
and go without her.

360 RODERIGO   Wilt thou be fast to my hopes, if I depend on
the issue?

IAGO   Thou art sure of me. Go, make money. I have told
thee often, and I retell thee again and again, I hate the
364 Moor. My cause is hearted; thine hath no less reason.
365 Let us be conjunctive in our revenge against him. If
366 thou canst cuckold him, thou dost thyself a pleasure,
me a sport. There are many events in the womb of
368 time, which will be delivered. Traverse, go, provide thy
money! We will have more of this tomorrow. Adieu.

370 RODERIGO   Where shall we meet i' th' morning?

IAGO   At my lodging.

372 RODERIGO   I'll be with thee betimes.

373 IAGO   Go to, farewell. – Do you hear, Roderigo?

RODERIGO   I'll sell all my land.   *Exit.*

IAGO

Thus do I ever make my fool my purse;
For I mine own gained knowledge should profane
377 If I would time expend with such a snipe
But for my sport and profit. I hate the Moor,

---

352 *delicate* pleasant; *Make* raise   353 *sanctimony* holiness (here false virtue
or faithfulness?)   354 *erring* wandering   356 *A pox of* i.e., "a curse on," "to
hell with" (*pox*=venereal disease)   357 *clean out of the way* i.e., out of the
question   357–59 *Seek thou . . . without her* i.e., risk death in trying to win
her rather than die and have no chance   360 *fast* faithful   360–61 *depend
on the issue* i.e., wait to see the outcome   364 *hearted* i.e., lodged deep in my
heart   365 *conjunctive* united   366 *cuckold him* commit adultery with his
wife   368 *Traverse* i.e., get moving, onward   372 *betimes* early   373 *Go to*
(conventional expression of impatience or agreement – "all right, then" or
"you see")   377 *snipe* dupe, fool

And it is thought abroad that 'twixt my sheets
H'as done my office. I know not if't be true,   380
But I, for mere suspicion in that kind,
Will do as if for surety. He holds me well;   382
The better shall my purpose work on him.
Cassio's a proper man. Let me see now: 384
To get his place, and to plume up my will   385
In double knavery – How, how? – Let's see: –
After some time, to abuse Othello's ears
That he is too familiar with his wife.
He hath a person and a smooth dispose   389
To be suspected – framed to make women false.   390
The Moor is of a free and open nature   391
That thinks men honest that but seem to be so;
And will as tenderly be led by th' nose
As asses are.
I have't! It is engendered! Hell and night
Must bring this monstrous birth to the world's light.
                                                          [Exit.]

                               *

∾ II.1 *Enter Montano and two Gentlemen.*

MONTANO
    What from the cape can you discern at sea?
FIRST GENTLEMAN
    Nothing at all: it is a high-wrought flood.   2
    I cannot 'twixt the heaven and the main   3
    Descry a sail.   4

---

380 *office* business (i.e., sexual)   382 *holds me well* thinks highly of me   384
proper (1) good-looking, (2) dutiful, responsible   385 *place* position, job;
plume up my will i.e., pride myself on getting what I want (*to plume* is to
show self-satisfaction, to preen)   389 *dispose* manner   391 *free* unreserved,
unsuspicious
    II.1 Cyprus, near the harbor   2 *high-wrought flood* turbulent sea   3
main sea   4 *Descry* discern, make out

MONTANO
 Methinks the wind hath spoke aloud at land;
 A fuller blast ne'er shook our battlements.
 If it hath ruffianed so upon the sea,
8 What ribs of oak, when mountains melt on them,
9 Can hold the mortise? What shall we hear of this?
SECOND [GENTLEMAN]
10 A segregation of the Turkish fleet.
 For do but stand upon the foaming shore,
12 The chidden billow seems to pelt the clouds;
13 The wind-shaked surge, with high and monstrous
  mane,
14 Seems to cast water on the burning Bear
15 And quench the Guards of th' ever-fixèd pole.
16 I never did like molestation view
17 On the enchafèd flood.
MONTANO   If that the Turkish fleet
 Be not ensheltered and embayed, they are drowned;
 It is impossible to bear it out.
  Enter a [third] Gentleman.
THIRD [GENTLEMAN]
20 News, lads! Our wars are done.
 The desperate tempest hath so banged the Turks
22 That their designment halts. A noble ship of Venice
23 Hath seen a grievous wrack and sufferance
 On most part of their fleet.
MONTANO
 How? Is this true?
THIRD [GENTLEMAN] The ship is here put in,

---

8 *ribs of oak* curved frame of a ship's hull 9 *hold the mortise* hold their joints
together 10 *segregation* scattering (i.e., defeat) 12 *chidden billow* i.e.,
driven wave (past tense of "chide," to scold or compel by scolding) 13
mane (figuratively the foam of the *surge* is like a monster's mane; with a pun
on "main," sea) 14 *burning Bear* constellation Ursa Minor 15 *Guards . . .
pole* two attendant stars, known as the "guardians" of the polestar 16 *molestation* turmoil 17 *enchafèd* furious, enraged 22 *designment halts* naval
plan limps 23 *wrack and sufferance* devastation and injury

A Veronesa. Michael Cassio,   26
Lieutenant to the warlike Moor, Othello,
Is come on shore; the Moor himself at sea,
And is in full commission here for Cyprus.

MONTANO
I am glad on't. 'Tis a worthy governor.   30

THIRD [GENTLEMAN]
But this same Cassio, though he speak of comfort   31
Touching the Turkish loss, yet he looks sadly
And prays the Moor be safe, for they were parted
With foul and violent tempest.

MONTANO   Pray heavens he be;
For I have served him, and the man commands
Like a full soldier. Let's to the seaside – ho! –
As well to see the vessel that's come in
As to throw out our eyes for brave Othello,
Even till we make the main and th' aerial blue   39
An indistinct regard.   40

GENTLEMAN   Come, let's do so;
For every minute is expectancy
Of more arrivance.
    Enter Cassio.

CASSIO
Thanks, you the valiant of the warlike isle,
That so approve the Moor! O, let the heavens   44
Give him defense against the elements,
For I have lost him on a dangerous sea!

MONTANO
Is he well shipped?

CASSIO
His bark is stoutly timbered, and his pilot
Of very expert and approved allowance;

---

26 *Veronesa* (probably a ship supplied by the city of Verona, but perhaps a
particular kind of vessel) 31 *of comfort* i.e., with relief 39–40 *Even till* . . .
regard until we can't distinguish the blues of sea and sky 44 *approve* admire,
support

50 Therefore my hopes, not surfeited to death,
    Stand in bold cure.
    [VOICES] *(Within)* A sail, a sail, a sail!
    CASSIO
    What noise?
    GENTLEMAN
    The town is empty; on the brow o' th' sea
    Stand ranks of people, and they cry "A sail!"
    CASSIO
55 My hopes do shape him for the governor.
        [A shot.]
    GENTLEMAN
    They do discharge their shot of courtesy:
    Our friends at least.
    CASSIO   I pray you, sir, go forth
    And give us truth who 'tis that is arrived.
    GENTLEMAN
    I shall.   *Exit.*
    MONTANO
60 But, good lieutenant, is your general wived?
    CASSIO
    Most fortunately. He hath achieved a maid
62 That paragons description and wild fame;
63 One that excels the quirks of blazoning pens,
64 And in th' essential vesture of creation
    Does tire the ingener.
        Enter Gentleman.
                            How now? Who has put in?
    GENTLEMAN
    'Tis one Iago, ancient to the general.

50–51 *my hopes . . . bold cure* i.e., since I haven't allowed myself to hope too
much (*hopes, not surfeited to death*), the chances of my getting my wish are
good (*Stand in bold cure*) **55** *My . . . governor* i.e., "I hope this is Othello's
ship" **62** *paragons . . . fame* surpasses the wildest praise **63** *quirks* turns of
phrase; *blazoning* descriptive (with the suggestion of praise) **64–65** *essential
vesture . . . ingener* i.e., her native excellence wearies the would-be inventor
(*ingener*) of praise

CASSIO
  H'as had most favorable and happy speed: 67
  Tempests themselves, high seas, and howling winds,
  The guttered rocks and congregated sands,   69
  Traitors ensteeped to enclog the guiltless keel,   70
  As having sense of beauty, do omit
  Their mortal natures, letting go safely by   72
  The divine Desdemona.
MONTANO   What is she?
CASSIO
  She that I spake of, our great captain's captain,
  Left in the conduct of the bold Iago,
  Whose footing here anticipates our thoughts   76
  A sennight's speed. Great Jove, Othello guard,   77
  And swell his sail with thine own pow'rful breath,
  That he may bless this bay with his tall ship,   79
  Make love's quick pants in Desdemona's arms,   80
  Give renewed fire to our extincted spirits,   81
  And bring all Cyprus comfort!
      *Enter Desdemona, Iago, Roderigo, and Emilia [with
      Attendants].*   O, behold!
  The riches of the ship is come on shore!
  You men of Cyprus, let her have your knees.   84
  Hail to thee, lady! and the grace of heaven,
  Before, behind thee, and on every hand,
  Enwheel thee round!
DESDEMONA   I thank you, valiant Cassio.
  What tidings can you tell me of my lord?
CASSIO
  He is not yet arrived, nor know I aught
  But that he's well and will be shortly here.   90

---

67 *happy speed* good fortune (as well as pace) 69 *guttered* grooved, jagged
70 *ensteeped* submerged 72 *mortal* deadly 76 *footing* landing 77 *sennight's* week's 79–80 *That . . . Make love's quick pants* i.e., that he may experience the rapid breathing of joyous love 81 *extincted* extinguished,
dampened 84 *let her have your knees* i.e., bow to her

DESDEMONA
    O but I fear! How lost you company?
CASSIO
    The great contention of sea and skies
    Parted our fellowship.
[VOICES] *(Within)* A sail, a sail! *[A shot.]*
CASSIO   But hark. A sail!
GENTLEMAN
    They give their greeting to the citadel;
    This likewise is a friend.
CASSIO   See for the news.
                                [Exit Gentleman.]
    Good ancient, you are welcome.
        [To Emilia]   Welcome, mistress. –
    Let it not gall your patience, good Iago,
98 That I extend my manners. 'Tis my breeding
99 That gives me this bold show of courtesy.
        [Kisses Emilia.]
IAGO
100 Sir, would she give you so much of her lips
101 As of her tongue she oft bestows on me,
    You would have enough.
DESDEMONA   Alas, she has no speech!
IAGO
    In faith, too much.
104 I find it still when I have leave to sleep.
    Marry, before your ladyship, I grant,
106 She puts her tongue a little in her heart
    And chides with thinking.
EMILIA
    You have little cause to say so.

---

98 *extend my manners* i.e., as far as Emilia   **99 s.d.** *Kisses Emilia* (a social custom among the Elizabethans)   **101** *tongue* (in the sense of scolding)   **104**
still always (i.e., even); *have leave* am allowed (and should be able)   **106–7**
She puts . . . thinking i.e., she scolds me silently

IAGO

   Come on, come on! You are pictures out of door,

   Bells in your parlors, wildcats in your kitchens,   110

   Saints in your injuries, devils being offended,   111

   Players in your huswifery, and huswives in your beds.   112

DESDEMONA

   O, fie upon thee, slanderer!

IAGO

   Nay, it is true, or else I am a Turk:

   You rise to play, and go to bed to work.

EMILIA

   You shall not write my praise.

IAGO   No, let me not.

DESDEMONA

   What wouldst write of me, if thou shouldst praise me?

IAGO

   O gentle lady, do not put me to't,

   For I am nothing if not critical.

DESDEMONA

   Come on, assay. – There's one gone to the harbor?   120

IAGO

   Ay, madam.

DESDEMONA

   I am not merry; but I do beguile   122

   The thing I am by seeming otherwise. –   123

   Come, how wouldst thou praise me?

IAGO

   I am about it; but indeed my invention   125

---

110 *Bells* i.e., noisemakers 111 *Saints in your injuries* i.e., pretenders of innocence when harming others 112 *Players in your huswifery* actors (i.e., not real workers at your housekeeping); *huswives in your beds* i.e., (1) in control of your husbands, (2) hussies, wantons 120 *assay* try 122 *beguile* charm away 123 *The thing I am* i.e., my nervousness about my husband's arrival 125 *invention* idea (i.e., the praise)

126   Comes from my pate as birdlime does from frieze –
       It plucks out brains and all. But my muse labors,
       And thus she is delivered:
       If she be fair and wise, fairness and wit –
130   The one's for use, the other useth it.

DESDEMONA

131   Well praised! How if she be black and witty?

IAGO

       If she be black, and thereto have a wit,
133   She'll find a white that shall her blackness fit.

DESDEMONA

       Worse and worse!

EMILIA

       How if fair and foolish?

IAGO

       She never yet was foolish that was fair,
137   For even her folly helped her to an heir.

138 DESDEMONA   These are old fond paradoxes to make
       fools laugh i' th' alehouse. What miserable praise hast
140   thou for her that's foul and foolish?

IAGO

       There's none so foul, and foolish thereunto,
       But does foul pranks which fair and wise ones do.

143 DESDEMONA   O heavy ignorance! Thou praisest the
       worst best. But what praise couldst thou bestow on a
       deserving woman indeed – one that in the authority of
146   her merit did justly put on the vouch of very malice it-
       self?

---

126 *pate* head; *as birdlime . . . frieze* with as much difficulty as getting *birdlime* (a sticky white paste used to trap birds) out of *frieze* (a coarse woolen cloth)   131 *black* brunet or dark-complexioned   133 *find a white . . . fit* (a complex pun: *white* = "wight" or "man," but also the "white" was the center of a target – i.e., "she'll find a matching fair-skinned man who likes her dark skin")   137 *folly* sexual looseness (as well as foolishness)   138 *fond* foolish   140 *foul* ugly   143 *heavy* grievous   146 *put on the vouch* win the approval

IAGO

  She that was ever fair, and never proud;
  Had tongue at will, and yet was never loud;
  Never lacked gold, and yet went never gay;   150
  Fled from her wish, and yet said "Now I may";   151
  She that, being angered, her revenge being nigh,
  Bade her wrong stay, and her displeasure fly;   153
  She that in wisdom never was so frail
  To change the cod's head for the salmon's tail;   155
  She that could think, and ne'er disclose her mind;
  See suitors following, and not look behind:
  She was a wight (if ever such wights were) –   158

DESDEMONA   To do what?

IAGO

  To suckle fools and chronicle small beer.   160

DESDEMONA   O most lame and impotent conclusion!
  Do not learn of him, Emilia, though he be thy husband. How say you, Cassio? Is he not a most profane   163
  and liberal counselor?

CASSIO   He speaks home, madam. You may relish him   165
  more in the soldier than in the scholar.

IAGO   *[Aside]* He takes her by the palm. Ay, well said,   167
  whisper! With as little a web as this will I ensnare as
  great a fly as Cassio. Ay, smile upon her, do! I will gyve   169
  thee in thine own courtship. – You say true; 'tis so, in-   170
  deed! – If such tricks as these strip you out of your lieu-
  tenantry, it had been better you had not kissed your

---

150 *gay* extravagantly dressed   151 *Fled . . . I may* i.e., did not allow herself
to do what she could have   153 *Bade her . . . fly* i.e., put up with her trouble
and dismissed her anger about it   155 *To change . . . tail* i.e., not so foolish
(*never . . . so frail*) as to exchange something worthless – *the cod's head* – for
something precious – *the salmon's tail* (*cod* [scrotum] and *tail* also have sexual
connotations)   158 *wight* person   160 *suckle* take care of; *chronicle small
beer* keep a tally of trivialities   163–64 *profane and liberal* lewd and free-
talking   165 *home* bluntly   167 *well said* i.e., well done, good work   169–
70 *gyve thee* chain you up, entrap you

three fingers so oft – which now again you are most apt
174　to play the sir in. Very good! well kissed! and excellent
courtesy! 'Tis so, indeed. Yet again your fingers to your
176　lips? Would they were clyster pipes for your sake!
[Trumpet within.] The Moor! I know his trumpet.
CASSIO　'Tis truly so.
DESDEMONA　Let's meet him and receive him.
180　CASSIO　Lo, where he comes.
　　　Enter Othello and Attendants.
OTHELLO
　O my fair warrior!
DESDEMONA　　　　　　My dear Othello!
OTHELLO
　It gives me wonder great as my content
　To see you here before me. O my soul's joy!
　If after every tempest come such calms,
　May the winds blow till they have wakened death!
　And let the laboring bark climb hills of seas
　Olympus-high, and duck again as low
188　As hell's from heaven! If it were now to die,
189　'Twere now to be most happy, for I fear
190　My soul hath her content so absolute
191　That not another comfort like to this
　Succeeds in unknown fate.
DESDEMONA　　　　　　　The heavens forbid
　But that our loves and comforts should increase
　Even as our days do grow.
OTHELLO　　　　　　Amen to that, sweet powers!
　I cannot speak enough of this content;
196　It stops me here; it is too much of joy.
　And this, and this, the greatest discords be
　　[They kiss.]
　That e'er our hearts shall make!

---

174 *play the sir in* act the courtier　176 *clyster pipes* tubes for enemas or vagi-
nal insertions　188 *If it were now* if it were now my fate　189 *happy* fortunate　191 *comfort* satisfaction　196 *here* (presumably he indicates his heart)

IAGO   *[Aside]*   O, you are well tuned now!
But I'll set down the pegs that make this music,   199
As honest as I am.   200
OTHELLO   Come, let us to the castle.
News, friends! Our wars are done; the Turks are
  drowned.
How does my old acquaintance of this isle? –
Honey, you shall be well desired in Cyprus;   203
I have found great love amongst them. O my sweet,
I prattle out of fashion, and I dote   205
In mine own comforts. I prithee, good Iago,
Go to the bay and disembark my coffers.   207
Bring thou the master to the citadel;   208
He is a good one, and his worthiness
Does challenge much respect. – Come, Desdemona,   210
Once more well met at Cyprus.
                        Exit Othello and Desdemona
                        [with all but Iago and Roderigo].
IAGO   *[To an Attendant going out]* Do thou meet me
presently at the harbor. *[To Roderigo]* Come hither. If
thou be'st valiant (as they say base men being in love
have then a nobility in their natures more than is native
to them), list me. The lieutenant tonight watches on   216
the court of guard. First, I must tell thee this. Desdemona is directly in love with him.
RODERIGO   With him? Why, 'tis not possible.
IAGO   Lay thy finger thus, and let thy soul be instructed. 220
Mark me with what violence she first loved the Moor,
but for bragging and telling her fantastical lies. To love
him still for prating? Let not thy discreet heart think it. 223
Her eye must be fed; and what delight shall she have to

---

199 *set down* i.e., loosen, untune   203 *well desired* sought after, welcomed
205 *out of fashion* i.e., as I shouldn't at this time   207 *disembark my coffers*
bring my luggage ashore (*coffers*= trunks)   208 *master* i.e., ship master   210
challenge demand, deserve   216 *list* listen to   216–17 *watches . . . guard* i.e.,
is on duty with the *corps de garde,* the patrol assigned to headquarters   220
thus i.e., on your lips, for silence   223 *discreet* discerning

225 look on the devil? When the blood is made dull with
226 the act of sport, there should be, again to inflame it and
227 to give satiety a fresh appetite, loveliness in favor, sympathy in years, manners, and beauties; all which the
Moor is defective in. Now for want of these required
230 conveniences, her delicate tenderness will find itself
231 abused, begin to heave the gorge, disrelish and abhor
the Moor. Very nature will instruct her in it and compel her to some second choice. Now sir, this granted –
234 as it is a most pregnant and unforced position – who
stands so eminent in the degree of this fortune as Cas-
236 sio does? A knave very voluble; no further conscionable
than in putting on the mere form of civil and humane
seeming for the better compass of his salt and most hid-
239 den loose affection? Why, none! why, none! A slipper
240 and subtle knave, a finder of occasion, that has an eye
241 can stamp and counterfeit advantages, though true advantage never present itself; a devilish knave! Besides,
the knave is handsome, young, and hath all those req-
244 uisites in him that folly and green minds look after. A
pestilent complete knave! and the woman hath found
him already.
RODERIGO   I cannot believe that in her; she's full of most
248 blessed condition.
249 IAGO   Blessed fig's-end! The wine she drinks is made of
250 grapes. If she had been blessed, she would never have
251 loved the Moor. Blessed pudding! Didst thou not see

---

225 *the devil* (traditionally represented as dark)   226 *act of sport* i.e., copula-
tion   227 *favor* appearance, especially of the face   230 *conveniences* points
of agreement (literally, "comings together")   231 *heave the gorge* vomit   234
pregnant apparent   236 *voluble* smooth-talking (also "inconstant")   236–
39 *no . . . affection* i.e., his conscience requires him to do no more than to assume good manners (*form of civil and humane seeming*) in order to succeed
sexually (*salt*=salacious, sexy)   239 *slipper* slippery   240 *finder of occasion*
i.e., an opportunist   241 *stamp . . . advantages* invent opportunities by
fraudulent (*counterfeit*) means   244 *green* young, naive; *look after* i.e., go for
248 *blessed condition* holy character   249 *fig's-end* (a crude turn on the pre-
ceding phrase; see I.3.319)   251 *pudding* sausage

her paddle with the palm of his hand? Didst not mark
that?

RODERIGO   Yes, that I did; but that was but courtesy.

IAGO   Lechery, by this hand! an index and obscure pro-   255
logue to the history of lust and foul thoughts. They met
so near with their lips that their breaths embraced together. Villainous thoughts, Roderigo! When these mu-   258
tualities so marshal the way, hard at hand comes the
master and main exercise, th' incorporate conclusion.   260
Pish! But, sir, be you ruled by me: I have brought you   261
from Venice. Watch you tonight. For the command, I'll   262
lay't upon you. Cassio knows you not. I'll not be far   263
from you: do you find some occasion to anger Cassio,
either by speaking too loud, or tainting his discipline,   265
or from what other course you please which the time
shall more favorably minister.

RODERIGO   Well.

IAGO   Sir, he's rash and very sudden in choler, and haply   269
may strike at you. Provoke him that he may; for even   270
out of that will I cause these of Cyprus to mutiny;   271
whose qualification shall come into no true taste again   272
but by the displanting of Cassio. So shall you have a
shorter journey to your desires by the means I shall
then have to prefer them; and the impediment most   275
profitably removed without the which there were no
expectation of our prosperity.

---

255 *an index* a table of contents; *obscure* hidden, secret   258–60 *mutualities . . . conclusion* polite exchanges (*mutualities*) initiate a figurative parade,
with hand-kissing as those who lead (*marshal the way*) followed immediately
(*hard at hand*) by the main event (*master and main exercise*), the sexual act
(*incorporate conclusion*)   261 *Pish* (expression of disgust)   262 *Watch you*
i.e., you join the watch   263 *lay't upon you* i.e., arrange for your participa-
tion   265 *tainting his discipline* belittling his professionalism   269 *sudden in choler* quick to anger;   *haply* perhaps   270 *Provoke . . . may* i.e., do
something to ensure that he will   271 *mutiny* riot   272 *qualification . . .
taste* (a drinking metaphor concerning diluted or altered wine; i.e., the disturbed Cypriots won't be back to normal until Cassio is fired)   275 *prefer*
advance

RODERIGO   I will do this if you can bring it to any opportunity.

280   IAGO   I warrant thee. Meet me by and by at the citadel; I
must fetch his necessaries ashore. Farewell.

RODERIGO   Adieu.   *Exit.*

IAGO
    That Cassio loves her, I do well believe't;
284   That she loves him, 'tis apt and of great credit.
    The Moor, howbeit that I endure him not,
    Is of a constant, loving, noble nature,
    And I dare think he'll prove to Desdemona
    A most dear husband. Now I do love her too;
    Not out of absolute lust, though peradventure
290   I stand accountant for as great a sin,
291   But partly led to diet my revenge,
    For that I do suspect the lusty Moor
293   Hath leaped into my seat, the thought whereof
    Doth, like a poisonous mineral, gnaw my inwards,
    And nothing can or shall content my soul
    Till I am evened with him, wife for wife;
    Or failing so, yet that I put the Moor
    At least into a jealousy so strong
    That judgment cannot cure. Which thing to do,
300   If this poor trash of Venice, whom I trace
301   For his quick hunting, stand the putting on,
302   I'll have our Michael Cassio on the hip,
303   Abuse him to the Moor in the rank garb
    (For I fear Cassio with my nightcap too),
    Make the Moor thank me, love me, and reward me
306   For making him egregiously an ass

---

284 *apt* likely; *of great credit* easily credible   **290** *accountant* accountable
291 *diet* feed, nourish   **293** *leaped into my seat* i.e., done my (sexual) job
300 *trace* pursue (with a pun on *trash* earlier in the line)   **301** *For his quick hunting* i.e., because he goes after what I tell him to; *stand the putting on* tol-
erates my using him as I do   **302** *on the hip* i.e., where I want him (term
from wrestling)   **303** *rank garb* nasty fashion   **306** *egregiously* exceptionally,
spectacularly

And practicing upon his peace and quiet   307
Even to madness. 'Tis here, but yet confused: 308
Knavery's plain face is never seen till used.   *Exit.*

                                   ✲

∾ **II.2** *Enter Othello's Herald, with a proclamation.*

HERALD   It is Othello's pleasure, our noble and valiant
general, that, upon certain tidings now arrived, import-
ing the mere perdition of the Turkish fleet, every man   3
put himself into triumph; some to dance, some to
make bonfires, each man to what sport and revels his
addition leads him. For, besides these beneficial news, 6
it is the celebration of his nuptial. So much was his
pleasure should be proclaimed. All offices are open, and 8
there is full liberty of feasting from this present hour of
five till the bell have told eleven. Heaven bless the isle 10
of Cyprus and our noble general Othello!   *Exit.*

                                   ✲

∾ **II.3** *Enter Othello, Desdemona, Cassio, and
Attendants.*

OTHELLO
Good Michael, look you to the guard tonight.
Let's teach ourselves that honorable stop,
Not to outsport discretion.   3
CASSIO
Iago hath direction what to do;
But notwithstanding, with my personal eye
Will I look to't.
OTHELLO   Iago is most honest.

---

307 *practicing upon* plotting against 308 *yet* so far
   II.2 Cyprus, a public area 3 *mere perdition* total loss 6 *addition* rank,
position 8 *offices* military storehouses 10 *told* tolled (with pun on
"tell"=count)
   II.3 The area in front of the Cyprian castle 3 *outsport* overrun, violate

7   Michael, good night. Tomorrow with your earliest
       Let me have speech with you.
              [To Desdemona]   Come, my dear love.
       The purchase made, the fruits are to ensue;
10   That profit's yet to come 'tween me and you. –
       Good night.
              Exit [Othello with Desdemona and Attendants].
              Enter Iago.
CASSIO   Welcome, Iago. We must to the watch.
IAGO   Not this hour, lieutenant; 'tis not yet ten o' th'
14   clock. Our general cast us thus early for the love of his
       Desdemona, who let us not therefore blame. He hath
       not yet made wanton the night with her, and she is
       sport for Jove.
CASSIO   She's a most exquisite lady.
19 IAGO   And, I'll warrant her, full of game.
20 CASSIO   Indeed, she's a most fresh and delicate creature.
21 IAGO   What an eye she has! Methinks it sounds a parley
       to provocation.
CASSIO   An inviting eye, and yet methinks right modest.
24 IAGO   And when she speaks, is it not an alarum to love?
CASSIO   She is indeed perfection.
IAGO   Well, happiness to their sheets! Come, lieutenant,
27   I have a stoup of wine, and here without are a brace of
28   Cyprus gallants that would fain have a measure to the
       health of black Othello.
30 CASSIO   Not tonight, good Iago. I have very poor and
       unhappy brains for drinking. I could well wish courtesy
       would invent some other custom of entertainment.
IAGO   O, they are our friends. But one cup! I'll drink for
       you.

---

7 *with your earliest* at your earliest convenience   14 *cast* dismissed, "cast us
off"   19 *full of game* i.e., sexually eager   21–22 *a parley to provocation* a signal to a sexual encounter (a military metaphor)   24 *an alarum* a call (again,
a military signal)   27 *stoup* tankard, container; *brace* pair   28 *would . . .
measure* desire to drink a toast

CASSIO   I have drunk but one cup tonight, and that was
   craftily qualified too, and behold what innovation it   36
   makes here. I am unfortunate in the infirmity and dare
   not task my weakness with any more.   38
IAGO   What, man! 'Tis a night of revels: the gallants de-
   sire it.   40
CASSIO   Where are they?
IAGO   Here at the door; I pray you call them in.
CASSIO   I'll do't, but it dislikes me.   *Exit.*
IAGO
   If I can fasten but one cup upon him
   With that which he hath drunk tonight already,
   He'll be as full of quarrel and offense
   As my young mistress' dog. Now my sick fool
     Roderigo,
   Whom love hath turned almost the wrong side out,
   To Desdemona hath tonight caroused   49
   Potations pottle-deep; and he's to watch.   50
   Three else of Cyprus – noble swelling spirits,   51
   That hold their honors in a wary distance,   52
   The very elements of this warlike isle –   53
   Have I tonight flustered with flowing cups,
   And they watch too. Now, 'mongst this flock of drunk-
     ards
   Am I to put our Cassio in some action
   That may offend the isle.
       Enter Cassio, Montano, and Gentlemen [with Servants
       bringing wine].
                       But here they come.
   If consequence do but approve my dream,   58
   My boat sails freely, both with wind and stream.

---

36 *craftily qualified* carefully diluted; *innovation* disturbance, revolution   **38**
task endanger, overtax   **49–50** *caroused / Potations pottle-deep* drunk gulps to
the bottom of the *pottle* or cup   **51** *else* others; *swelling* proud   **52** *hold . . .*
distance are vain and sensitive about their honor   **53** *very elements* i.e.,
the proud soldiers represent the essential defensiveness of the islanders   **58** *con-*
sequence what follows; *approve* bear out

60 CASSIO 'Fore God, they have given me a rouse already.

MONTANO Good faith, a little one; not past a pint, as I
am a soldier.

IAGO Some wine, ho!
        [Sings.]

64   And let me the cannikin clink, clink;
                And let me the cannikin clink.
                    A soldier's a man;
                    O man's life's but a span,
                Why then, let a soldier drink.
        Some wine, boys!

70 CASSIO 'Fore God, an excellent song!

IAGO I learned it in England, where indeed they are
most potent in potting. Your Dane, your German, and
73 your swagbellied Hollander – Drink, ho! – are nothing
to your English.

75 CASSIO Is your Englishman so exquisite in his drinking?

76 IAGO Why, he drinks you with facility your Dane dead
77 drunk; he sweats not to overthrow your Almain; he
78 gives your Hollander a vomit ere the next pottle can be
filled.

80 CASSIO To the health of our general!

MONTANO I am for it, lieutenant, and I'll do you justice.

IAGO O sweet England!
        [Sings.]
                King Stephen was and-a worthy peer,
                    His breeches cost him but a crown;
                He held them sixpence all too dear,
86   With that he called the tailor lown.
                He was a wight of high renown,
                    And thou art but of low degree.

---

60 *a rouse* a carouse (i.e., a drink) 64 *cannikin* (diminutive of "can"); *clink*
i.e., against another in a toast 73 *swagbellied* with a stomach draped over
the belt 75 *exquisite* (1) accomplished, (2) extreme 76 *with facility* easily
77 *Almain* German (French *Allemagne*, Germany) 78 *gives . . . vomit* i.e.,
causes the Dutchman to throw up 86 *lown* rascal, lout

> 'Tis pride that pulls the country down;
>> Then take thine auld cloak about thee.   90

Some wine, ho!

CASSIO 'Fore God, this is a more exquisite song than the other.

IAGO Will you hear't again?

CASSIO No, for I hold him to be unworthy of his place that does those things. Well, God's above all; and there 96 be souls must be saved, and there be souls must not be saved.

IAGO It's true, good lieutenant.

CASSIO For mine own part – no offense to the general, 100 nor any man of quality – I hope to be saved.   101

IAGO And so do I too, lieutenant.

CASSIO Ay, but, by your leave, not before me. The lieutenant is to be saved before the ancient. Let's have no more of this; let's to our affairs. – God forgive us our sins! – Gentlemen, let's look to our business. Do not think, gentlemen, I am drunk. This is my ancient; this is my right hand, and this is my left. I am not drunk now. I can stand well enough, and I speak well enough.

GENTLEMEN Excellent well!   110

CASSIO Why, very well then. You must not think then that I am drunk.   *Exit.*

MONTANO
To th' platform, masters. Come, let's set the watch.
                              [Exeunt some Gentlemen.]

IAGO
You see this fellow that is gone before.   114
He's a soldier fit to stand by Caesar
And give direction, and do but see his vice.
'Tis to his virtue a just equinox,   117
The one as long as th' other. 'Tis pity of him.

---

90 *auld* old   **96** *does those things* behaves in that way   **101** *man of quality* person of high rank or station   **114** *fellow* person (but sometimes, perhaps here, with a contemptuous undertone); *is gone before* just left   **117** *just equinox* precise equivalent

I fear the trust Othello puts him in,
120   On some odd time of his infirmity,
Will shake this island.

MONTANO   But is he often thus?

IAGO
'Tis evermore his prologue to his sleep:
123   He'll watch the horologe a double set
If drink rock not his cradle.

MONTANO   It were well
The general were put in mind of it.
Perhaps he sees it not, or his good nature
Prizes the virtue that appears in Cassio
And looks not on his evils. Is not this true?
    Enter Roderigo.

IAGO   *[Aside to him]*
How now, Roderigo?
130   I pray you after the lieutenant, go!   *[Exit Roderigo.]*

MONTANO
And 'tis great pity that the noble Moor
Should hazard such a place as his own second
133   With one of an engraffed infirmity.
It were an honest action to say
So to the Moor.

IAGO   Not I, for this fair island!
I do love Cassio well and would do much
To cure him of this evil.

[VOICE]   *(Within)* Help! help!

IAGO   But hark! What noise?
    Enter Cassio pursuing Roderigo.

CASSIO
Zounds, you rogue! you rascal!

MONTANO
What's the matter, lieutenant?

123–24 *watch . . . cradle* stay awake twice around the clock unless he has
a drink (i.e., Cassio can't sleep without drinking first)   133 *an engraffed* a
built-in

CASSIO   A knave teach me my duty?
I'll beat the knave into a twiggen bottle.   140

RODERIGO
    Beat me?

CASSIO   Dost thou prate, rogue?
    [Strikes Roderigo.]

MONTANO   Nay, good lieutenant!
    [Stays Cassio.]
    I pray you, sir, hold your hand.

CASSIO   Let me go, sir,
Or I'll knock you o'er the mazard.   143

MONTANO   Come, come, you're
    drunk!

CASSIO   Drunk?
    [They fight.]

IAGO   *[Aside to Roderigo]*
    Away, I say! Go out and cry a mutiny! *[Exit Roderigo.]*
    Nay, good lieutenant. God's will, gentlemen!
    [A bell rung.]
    Help, ho! – lieutenant – sir – Montano!
    Help, masters! – Here's a goodly watch indeed!
    Who's that which rings the bell? Diablo, ho!   149
    The town will rise. God's will, lieutenant, hold!   150
    You'll be ashamed forever.
    Enter Othello and Attendants.

OTHELLO   What is the matter here?

MONTANO
    Zounds, I bleed still. I am hurt to th' death.
    He dies!

OTHELLO
    Hold for your lives!

IAGO
    Hold, ho! Lieutenant – sir – Montano – gentlemen!

---

140 *twiggen bottle* wicker-covered bottle (i.e., Cassio threatens crisscross
stripes on his victim's skin)   143 *mazard* head   149 *Diablo* devil (an oath)
150 *rise* i.e., rise up, riot

Have you forgot all place of sense and duty?
Hold! The general speaks to you. Hold, for shame!

OTHELLO
Why, how now, ho? From whence ariseth this?
159   Are we turned Turks, and to ourselves do that
160   Which heaven hath forbid the Ottomites?
For Christian shame put by this barbarous brawl!
162   He that stirs next to carve for his own rage
163   Holds his soul light; he dies upon his motion.
Silence that dreadful bell! It frights the isle
165   From her propriety. What is the matter, masters?
Honest Iago, that looks dead with grieving,
Speak. Who began this? On thy love, I charge thee.

IAGO
I do not know. Friends all, but now, even now,
169   In quarter, and in terms like bride and groom
170   Devesting them for bed; and then, but now –
As if some planet had unwitted men –
172   Swords out, and tilting one at others' breasts
In opposition bloody. I cannot speak
174   Any beginning to this peevish odds,
And would in action glorious I had lost
Those legs that brought me to a part of it!

OTHELLO
How comes it, Michael, you are thus forgot?

CASSIO
I pray you pardon me. I cannot speak.

OTHELLO
Worthy Montano, you were wont to be civil;
180   The gravity and stillness of your youth
The world hath noted, and your name is great

---

159 *Are . . . turned Turks* have we become barbarous (proverbial in the period)   160 *hath forbid the Ottomites* i.e., to defeat ourselves (which they
could not)   162 *carve for his own rage* indulge his anger   163 *Holds his soul
light* doesn't value his own soul (i.e., will die)   165 *propriety* proper state
(i.e., calm)   169 *quarter* conduct toward; *terms* language   172 *tilting* aim-
ing, thrusting   174 *peevish odds* headstrong, childish strife

In mouths of wisest censure. What's the matter   182
That you unlace your reputation thus   183
And spend your rich opinion for the name   184
Of a night brawler? Give me answer to it.

MONTANO
Worthy Othello, I am hurt to danger.
Your officer, Iago, can inform you,
While I spare speech, which something now offends me,   188
Of all that I do know; nor know I aught
By me that's said or done amiss this night,   *190*
Unless self-charity be sometimes a vice,   191
And to defend ourselves it be a sin
When violence assails us.

OTHELLO   Now, by heaven,
My blood begins my safer guides to rule,   194
And passion, having my best judgment collied,   195
Assays to lead the way. Zounds, if I stir
Or do but lift this arm, the best of you
Shall sink in my rebuke. Give me to know
How this foul rout began, who set it on,
And he that is approved in this offense,   200
Though he had twinned with me, both at a birth,
Shall lose me. What! in a town of war,
Yet wild, the people's hearts brimful of fear,
To manage private and domestic quarrel?   204
In night, and on the court and guard of safety?
'Tis monstrous. Iago, who began't?

MONTANO
If partially affined, or leagued in office,   207
Thou dost deliver more or less than truth,

---

182 *censure* judgment   183 *unlace* undo, remove   184 *spend your rich opin-*
ion squander your reputation   188 *something now offends me* i.e., somewhat
pains me, is difficult for me   191 *self-charity* self-protection   194 *blood* passion (as elsewhere in the play)   195 *collied* darkened, obscured (covered with
coal dust?)   200 *approved in* found guilty of   204 *manage* conduct   207
partially . . . office bound by partiality or soldierly affiliation

209   Thou art no soldier.
         IAGO   Touch me not so near.
210   I had rather have this tongue cut from my mouth
         Than it should do offense to Michael Cassio;
         Yet I persuade myself, to speak the truth
         Shall nothing wrong him. This it is, general.
         Montano and myself being in speech,
         There comes a fellow crying out for help
         And Cassio following him with determined sword
217   To execute upon him. Sir, this gentleman
         Steps in to Cassio and entreats his pause.
         Myself the crying fellow did pursue,
220   Lest by his clamor (as it so fell out)
         The town might fall in fright. He, swift of foot,
         Outran my purpose; and I returned then rather
         For that I heard the clink and fall of swords,
224   And Cassio high in oath; which till tonight
         I ne'er might say before. When I came back –
         For this was brief – I found them close together
         At blow and thrust, even as again they were
         When you yourself did part them.
         More of this matter cannot I report.
230   But men are men; the best sometimes forget.
         Though Cassio did some little wrong to him,
         As men in rage strike those that wish them best,
         Yet surely Cassio I believe received
         From him that fled some strange indignity,
235   Which patience could not pass.
         OTHELLO   I know, Iago,
236   Thy honesty and love doth mince this matter,
237   Making it light to Cassio. Cassio, I love thee,

---

209 *Touch* charge   **217** *execute upon* take action against   **224** *high in oath*
in a fit of cursing   **235** *pass* i.e., pass over, let go by   **236** *love* i.e., affection
for your colleague; *mince* reduce, minimize   **237** *love* respect and feel affection for

But never more be officer of mine.
 Enter Desdemona, attended.
Look if my gentle love be not raised up!
I'll make thee an example.   *240*

DESDEMONA
What is the matter, dear?   *241*

OTHELLO   All's well, sweeting.
Come away to bed. *[To Montano]* Sir, for your hurts,
Myself will be your surgeon. Lead him off.
         [Montano is led off.]
Iago, look with care about the town
And silence those whom this vile brawl distracted. *245*
Come, Desdemona, 'tis the soldiers' life
To have their balmy slumbers waked with strife.
      Exit [with all but Iago and Cassio].

IAGO What, are you hurt, lieutenant?

CASSIO Ay, past all surgery.

IAGO Marry, God forbid!   *250*

CASSIO Reputation, reputation, reputation! O, I have
lost my reputation! I have lost the immortal part of myself, and what remains is bestial. My reputation, Iago,
my reputation!

IAGO As I am an honest man, I had thought you had received some bodily wound. There is more sense in that *256*
than in reputation. Reputation is an idle and most false
imposition, oft got without merit and lost without de- *258*
serving. You have lost no reputation at all unless you re-
pute yourself such a loser. What, man! there are more *260*
ways to recover the general again. You are but now cast *261*
in his mood – a punishment more in policy than in *262*

---

241 *sweeting* sweetheart 245 *distracted* excited, disturbed 256 *sense* material reality 258 *imposition* something imposed from without 261 *recover
the general* i.e., recuperate your standing with Othello 261–62 *cast in his
mood* dismissed owing to his anger 262 *in policy* i.e., a strategic punishment

263 malice, even so as one would beat his offenseless dog to
264 affright an imperious lion. Sue to him again, and he's
yours.

CASSIO   I will rather sue to be despised than to deceive so
good a commander with so slight, so drunken, and so
268 indiscreet an officer. Drunk! and speak parrot! and
269 squabble! swagger! swear! and discourse fustian with
270 one's own shadow! O thou invisible spirit of wine, if
thou hast no name to be known by, let us call thee
devil!

IAGO   What was he that you followed with your sword?
What had he done to you?

CASSIO   I know not.

IAGO   Is't possible?

CASSIO   I remember a mass of things, but nothing dis-
278 tinctly; a quarrel, but nothing wherefore. O God, that
men should put an enemy in their mouths to steal away
280 their brains! that we should with joy, pleasance, revel,
281 and applause transform ourselves into beasts!

IAGO   Why, but you are now well enough. How came
you thus recovered?

CASSIO   It hath pleased the devil drunkenness to give
285 place to the devil wrath. One unperfectness shows me
another, to make me frankly despise myself.

IAGO   Come, you are too severe a moraler. As the time,
the place, and the condition of this country stands, I
could heartily wish this had not befall'n; but since it is
290 as it is, mend it for your own good.

CASSIO   I will ask him for my place again: he shall tell me
292 I am a drunkard! Had I as many mouths as Hydra, such

263–64 *beat . . . lion* i.e., make an example of you to frighten others   264
imperious powerful; *Sue to* petition   268 *speak parrot* babble idiotically   269
discourse fustian speak bombastic nonsense   278 *nothing wherefore* not why
281 *applause* approval (i.e., social approbation)   285 *unperfectness* failing
292 *Hydra* the legendary multiheaded monster

an answer would stop them all. To be now a sensible
man, by and by a fool, and presently a beast! O strange!
Every inordinate cup is unblessed, and the ingredient is   295
a devil.

IAGO   Come, come, good wine is a good familiar crea-   297
ture if it be well used. Exclaim no more against it. And,
good lieutenant, I think you think I love you.

CASSIO   I have well approved it, sir. I drunk!   300

IAGO   You or any man living may be drunk at a time,
man. I tell you what you shall do. Our general's wife is   302
now the general. I may say so in this respect, for that he
hath devoted and given up himself to the contempla-
tion, mark, and denotement of her parts and graces.   305
Confess yourself freely to her; importune her help to
put you in your place again. She is of so free, so kind, so   307
apt, so blessed a disposition she holds it a vice in her
goodness not to do more than she is requested. This
broken joint between you and her husband entreat her   310
to splinter; and my fortunes against any lay worth nam-   311
ing, this crack of your love shall grow stronger than it   312
was before.

CASSIO   You advise me well.

IAGO   I protest, in the sincerity of love and honest kind-   315
ness.

CASSIO   I think it freely; and betimes in the morning I
will beseech the virtuous Desdemona to undertake for   318
me. I am desperate of my fortunes if they check me   319
here.   320

---

295 *inordinate* immoderate   297–98 *familiar creature* friendly thing (but
with pun on *familiar* in the sense of an evil spirit)   300 *approved* demon-
strated, proved   302–3 *general's wife . . . general* i.e., Desdemona rules her
husband   305 *parts* gifts, abilities   307 *free* generous   310–11 *entreat her
to splinter* i.e., ask her to set with a splint   311 *lay* wager   312 *crack of* division in   315 *protest* affirm   318–19 *undertake for me* take up my plea   319
desperate of my fortunes in despair about my future; *check me* stop me

IAGO You are in the right. Good night, lieutenant; I
   must to the watch.

CASSIO Good night, honest Iago.   *Exit Cassio.*

IAGO
   And what's he then that says I play the villain,
   When this advice is free I give and honest,
326   Probal to thinking, and indeed the course
   To win the Moor again? For 'tis most easy
328   Th' inclining Desdemona to subdue
329   In any honest suit; she's framed as fruitful
330   As the free elements. And then for her
331   To win the Moor – were't to renounce his baptism,
   All seals and symbols of redeemèd sin –
333   His soul is so enfettered to her love
   That she may make, unmake, do what she list,
335   Even as her appetite shall play the god
   With his weak function. How am I then a villain
337   To counsel Cassio to this parallel course,
338   Directly to his good? Divinity of hell!
339   When devils will the blackest sins put on,
340   They do suggest at first with heavenly shows,
   As I do now. For whiles this honest fool
342   Plies Desdemona to repair his fortune,
   And she for him pleads strongly to the Moor,
   I'll pour this pestilence into his ear,
345   That she repeals him for her body's lust;
   And by how much she strives to do him good,
   She shall undo her credit with the Moor.
   So will I turn her virtue into pitch,
   And out of her own goodness make the net

---

326 *Probal* plausible 328 *subdue* convince 329 *fruitful* generous 331–32
were't . . . redeemèd sin i.e., she could make him go as far as to renounce his
faith 333 *enfettered* bound, enslaved 335–36 *Even as . . . weak function*
i.e., he is helpless to deny whatever she wants 337 *parallel* similar, related
338 *Divinity* theology 339 *put on* bring about 342 *Plies* petitions 345
repeals i.e., tries to get him reinstated (literally, "recalls")

That shall enmesh them all.   350
    Enter Roderigo.   How, now, Roderigo?
RODERIGO I do follow here in the chase, not like a hound
that hunts, but one that fills up the cry. My money is   352
almost spent; I have been tonight exceedingly well   353
cudgeled; and I think the issue will be – I shall have so   354
much experience for my pains, and so, with no money
at all, and a little more wit, return again to Venice.

IAGO
How poor are they that have not patience!
What wound did ever heal but by degrees?
Thou know'st we work by wit and not by witchcraft,   359
And wit depends on dilatory time.   360
Does't not go well? Cassio hath beaten thee,
And thou by that small hurt hast cashiered Cassio.   362
Though other things grow fair against the sun,   363
Yet fruits that blossom first will first be ripe.
Content thyself awhile. By the mass, 'tis morning!
Pleasure and action make the hours seem short.
Retire thee; go where thou art billeted.   367
Away, I say! Thou shalt know more hereafter.
Nay, get thee gone!   *Exit Roderigo.*
             Two things are to be done:
My wife must move for Cassio to her mistress –   370
I'll set her on –
Myself a while to draw the Moor apart
And bring him jump when he may Cassio find   373
Soliciting his wife. Ay, that's the way!
Dull not device by coldness and delay.   *Exit.* 375

                         *

---

352 *cry* pack of dogs   354 *cudgeled* beaten (with a cudgel); *issue* outcome
359 *wit* cunning, mind   360 *dilatory* slow-moving, unfolding   362
cashiered dismissed (i.e., got him fired)   363–64 *Though . . . ripe* i.e., although it looks as if others are prospering, our plan (*fruits that blossom first*)
will soon bear fruit (*first be ripe*)   367 *billeted* assigned lodging   370 *move*
plead   373 *jump* just, exactly   375 *Dull not device* don't hold up the scheme

∾ **III.1** *Enter Cassio, Musicians, and Clown.*

CASSIO

1   Masters, play here, I will content your pains:
Something that's brief; and bid "Good morrow, general."
[They play.]

3 CLOWN Why, masters, have your instruments been in
Naples, that they speak i' th' nose thus?

MUSICIAN How, sir, how?

6 CLOWN Are these, I pray you, wind instruments?

MUSICIAN Ay, marry, are they, sir.

CLOWN O, thereby hangs a tail.

MUSICIAN Whereby hangs a tale, sir?

10 CLOWN Marry, sir, by many a wind instrument that I
know. But, masters, here's money for you; and the general so likes your music that he desires you, for love's
sake, to make no more noise with it.

MUSICIAN Well, sir, we will not.

CLOWN If you have any music that may not be heard,
to't again: but, as they say, to hear music the general
does not greatly care.

18 MUSICIAN We have none such, sir.

CLOWN Then put up your pipes in your bag, for I'll

20 away. Go, vanish into air, away!   *Exit Musicians.*

CASSIO Dost thou hear, mine honest friend?

CLOWN No, I hear not your honest friend. I hear you.

23 CASSIO Prithee keep up thy quillets. There's a poor piece
of gold for thee. If the gentlewoman that attends the

25 general's wife be stirring, tell her there's one Cassio en-
treats her a little favor of speech. Wilt thou do this?

III.1 The grounds of the castle   **1** *content your pains* reward you for your labor
3–4 *in Naples . . . thus* i.e., why do your musical instruments whine so (Have
they been in Naples, associated with venereal disease, and caught syphilis, thus
causing their noses to fall off and produce such a sound?)   **6** *wind instruments*
(the following lines initiate a series of puns on *wind*, or *tail*) **18** *none such* ("Nonesuch" was the name of a popular tune)   **23** *keep up* put
away; *quillets* quips, jokes   **25** *be stirring* i.e., is moving around, awake

CLOWN   She is stirring, sir. If she will stir hither, I shall
seem to notify unto her.

CASSIO
Do, good my friend.   *Exit Clown.*   29
    Enter Iago.   In happy time, Iago.

IAGO
You have not been abed then?   *30*

CASSIO
Why, no; the day had broke
Before we parted. I have made bold, Iago,
To send in to your wife. My suit to her
Is that she will to virtuous Desdemona
Procure me some access.

IAGO   I'll send her to you presently,
And I'll devise a mean to draw the Moor   *36*
Out of the way, that your converse and business
May be more free.

CASSIO
I humbly thank you for't.   *Exit [Iago].*
                          I never knew
A Florentine more kind and honest.   *40*
    Enter Emilia.

EMILIA
Good morrow, good lieutenant. I am sorry
For your displeasure, but all will sure be well.
The general and his wife are talking of it,
And she speaks for you stoutly. The Moor replies   *44*
That he you hurt is of great fame in Cyprus
And great affinity, and that in wholesome wisdom   *46*
He might not but refuse you; but he protests he loves
    you,

---

29 *happy* fortunate (i.e., "good to see you")   **36** *devise a mean* invent a way
40 *Florentine . . . honest* i.e., even my own countrymen aren't so honest (Cassio comes from Florence, Iago from Venice, notorious for trickery)   **44**
stoutly strongly   **46** *great affinity* i.e., is well-connected   **46–47** *in wholesome . . . refuse you* i.e., common sense forbids him to reinstate you

48   And needs no other suitor but his likings
      To bring you in again.

CASSIO   Yet I beseech you,
50   If you think fit, or that it may be done,
      Give me advantage of some brief discourse
      With Desdemon alone.

EMILIA   Pray you come in.
      I will bestow you where you shall have time
54   To speak your bosom freely.

CASSIO   I am much bound to you.
                               [Exeunt.]

             *

∾ **III.2** *Enter Othello, Iago, and Gentlemen.*

OTHELLO
      These letters give, Iago, to the pilot
      And by him do my duties to the Senate.
3   That done, I will be walking on the works;
4   Repair there to me.

IAGO   Well, my good lord, I'll do't.

OTHELLO
      This fortification, gentlemen, shall we see't?

GENTLEMEN
      We'll wait upon your lordship.   *Exeunt.*

             *

∾ **III.3** *Enter Desdemona, Cassio, and Emilia.*

DESDEMONA
      Be thou assured, good Cassio, I will do
      All my abilities in thy behalf.

---

48 *no . . . likings* i.e., his own inclination would be sufficient by itself   54
bosom i.e., inmost feelings
    III.2 The grounds of the castle   3 *works* breastworks, fortifications   4
Repair return
    III.3 The grounds of the castle

EMILIA
    Good madam, do. I warrant it grieves my husband
    As if the cause were his.

DESDEMONA
    O, that's an honest fellow. Do not doubt, Cassio,
    But I will have my lord and you again
    As friendly as you were.

CASSIO   Bounteous madam,
    Whatever shall become of Michael Cassio,
    He's never anything but your true servant.

DESDEMONA
    I know't; I thank you. You do love my lord;   10
    You have known him long; and be you well assured
    He shall in strangeness stand no farther off   12
    Than in a politic distance.   13

CASSIO   Ay, but, lady,
    That policy may either last so long,
    Or feed upon such nice and waterish diet,   15
    Or breed itself so out of circumstances,   16
    That, I being absent, and my place supplied,   17
    My general will forget my love and service.

DESDEMONA
    Do not doubt that. Before Emilia here   19
    I give thee warrant of thy place. Assure thee,   20
    If I do vow a friendship, I'll perform it
    To the last article. My lord shall never rest;
    I'll watch him tame and talk him out of patience;   23
    His bed shall seem a school, his board a shrift;   24
    I'll intermingle everything he does
    With Cassio's suit. Therefore be merry, Cassio,
    For thy solicitor shall rather die

---

12 *strangeness* aloofness 13 *Than . . . distance* than wise policy demands
15 *feed . . . diet* i.e., have so little to nourish it 16 *breed . . . circumstances*
i.e., get so far away from the original point 17 *place supplied* position filled
by someone else 19 *doubt* suspect, fear 23 *watch him tame* i.e., keep him
awake until he does what I want 24 *board a shrift* i.e., his dining table will
seem a confessional (where he receives spiritual advice)

Than give thy cause away.
  Enter Othello and Iago [at a distance].

EMILIA
Madam, here comes my lord.

CASSIO
30 Madam, I'll take my leave.

DESDEMONA
Why, stay, and hear me speak.

CASSIO
Madam, not now: I am very ill at ease,
Unfit for mine own purposes.

DESDEMONA
Well, do your discretion.   *Exit Cassio.*

IAGO
Ha! I like not that.

OTHELLO   What dost thou say?

IAGO
Nothing, my lord; or if – I know not what.

OTHELLO
Was not that Cassio parted from my wife?

IAGO
Cassio, my lord? No, sure, I cannot think it,
That he would steal away so guiltylike,
40 Seeing your coming.

OTHELLO   I do believe 'twas he.

DESDEMONA
How now, my lord?
I have been talking with a suitor here,
A man that languishes in your displeasure.

OTHELLO
Who is't you mean?

DESDEMONA
Why, your lieutenant, Cassio. Good my lord,
If I have any grace or power to move you,
47 His present reconciliation take.

---

47 *His . . . take* immediately restore him to your good graces

For if he be not one that truly loves you,
That errs in ignorance, and not in cunning,
I have no judgment in an honest face.   50
I prithee call him back.
OTHELLO   Went he hence now?
DESDEMONA
Yes, faith; so humbled
That he hath left part of his grief with me
To suffer with him. Good love, call him back.
OTHELLO
Not now, sweet Desdemon; some other time.
DESDEMONA
But shall't be shortly?
OTHELLO   The sooner, sweet, for you.
DESDEMONA
Shall't be tonight at supper?
OTHELLO   No, not tonight.
DESDEMONA
Tomorrow dinner then?
OTHELLO   I shall not dine at home;
I meet the captains at the citadel.
DESDEMONA
Why then, tomorrow night, on Tuesday morn,   60
On Tuesday noon or night, on Wednesday morn.
I prithee name the time, but let it not
Exceed three days. In faith, he's penitent;
And yet his trespass, in our common reason   64
(Save that they say the wars must make example
Out of her best), is not almost a fault   66
T' incur a private check. When shall he come?   67
Tell me, Othello. I wonder in my soul
What you would ask me that I should deny
Or stand so mamm'ring on. What? Michael Cassio,   70

---

64 *in . . . reason* i.e., looked at by normal standards 66 *not almost* scarcely
67 *a private check* even a private reprimand 70 *mamm'ring on* hesitating
about or perhaps stuttering

That came a-wooing with you, and so many a time,
When I have spoke of you dispraisingly,
Hath ta'en your part – to have so much to do
74   To bring him in? By'r Lady, I could do much –
OTHELLO
Prithee no more. Let him come when he will!
76   I will deny thee nothing.
DESDEMONA   Why, this is not a boon;
'Tis as I should entreat you wear your gloves,
Or feed on nourishing dishes, or keep you warm,
79   Or sue to you to do a peculiar profit
80   To your own person. Nay, when I have a suit
81   Wherein I mean to touch your love indeed,
82   It shall be full of poise and difficult weight,
And fearful to be granted.
OTHELLO   I will deny thee nothing!
Whereon I do beseech thee grant me this,
To leave me but a little to myself.
DESDEMONA
Shall I deny you? No. Farewell, my lord.
OTHELLO
Farewell, my Desdemona: I'll come to thee straight.
DESDEMONA
88   Emilia, come. – Be as your fancies teach you;
Whate'er you be, I am obedient.   *Exit [with Emilia].*
OTHELLO
90   Excellent wretch! Perdition catch my soul
But I do love thee! and when I love thee not,
Chaos is come again.
IAGO
My noble lord –

---

74 *bring him in* i.e., into your favor 76 *boon* personal favor (i.e., I'm not asking you to do something for me, but rather for your own good) 79 *peculiar* particular, special 81 *touch* test 82–83 *full . . . granted* i.e., something hard to agree to 88 *as . . . you* i.e., as your whims suggest 90 *wretch* (a term of affection, but the opposite is also current in the period) 90–91 *Perdition . . . thee* i.e., I'll be damned if I don't love you

OTHELLO   What dost thou say, Iago?

IAGO
  Did Michael Cassio, when you wooed my lady,
  Know of your love?

OTHELLO
  He did, from first to last. Why dost thou ask?

IAGO
  But for a satisfaction of my thought;
  No further harm.

OTHELLO   Why of thy thought, Iago?

IAGO
  I did not think he had been acquainted with her.

OTHELLO
  O, yes, and went between us very oft.   100

IAGO
  Indeed?

OTHELLO
  Indeed? Ay, indeed! Discern'st thou aught in that?
  Is he not honest?

IAGO   Honest, my lord?

OTHELLO   Honest. Ay, honest.

IAGO
  My lord, for aught I know.

OTHELLO
  What dost thou think?

IAGO   Think, my lord?

OTHELLO   Think, my lord?
  By heaven, thou echo'st me
  As if there were some monster in thy thought
  Too hideous to be shown. Thou dost mean something:
  I heard thee say even now, thou lik'st not that,
  When Cassio left my wife. What didst not like?   110
  And when I told thee he was of my counsel   111
  In my whole course of wooing, thou cried'st "Indeed?"

---

100 *went between us* i.e., served as a go-between   111 *of my counsel* my confidant (i.e., knew my plans)

And didst contract and purse thy brow together,
As if thou then hadst shut up in thy brain
115   Some horrible conceit. If thou dost love me,
Show me thy thought.

IAGO
My lord, you know I love you.

OTHELLO   I think thou dost,
And, for I know thou'rt full of love and honesty
And weigh'st thy words before thou giv'st them breath,
120   Therefore these stops of thine fright me the more.
For such things in a false disloyal knave
122   Are tricks of custom, but in a man that's just
123   They're close dilations, working from the heart
That passion cannot rule.

IAGO   For Michael Cassio,
I dare be sworn I think that he is honest.

OTHELLO
I think so too.

IAGO   Men should be what they seem;
127   Or those that be not, would they might seem none!

OTHELLO
Certain, men should be what they seem.

IAGO
Why then, I think Cassio's an honest man.

OTHELLO
130   Nay, yet there's more in this.
I prithee speak to me as to thy thinkings,
As thou dost ruminate, and give thy worst of thoughts
The worst of words.

IAGO   Good my lord, pardon me:
Though I am bound to every act of duty,
I am not bound to that. All slaves are free –

---

115 *conceit* fancy or idea (Italian *concetto,* concept)   120 *stops* hesitations, re-
fusals   122 *tricks of custom* tricks of the trade; *just* honest, good   123 *close
dilations* secret swellings ("dilate"=expand) of emotion that can't be con-
trolled   127 *seem none* i.e., not pretend to be men but be instead the mon-
sters that they are

Utter my thoughts? Why, say they are vile and false,
As where's that palace whereinto foul things
Sometimes intrude not? Who has that breast so pure
But some uncleanly apprehensions   139
Keep leets and law days, and in sessions sit   140
With meditations lawful?

OTHELLO
Thou dost conspire against thy friend, Iago,
If thou but think'st him wronged, and mak'st his ear
A stranger to thy thoughts.

IAGO   I do beseech you –
Though I perchance am vicious in my guess
(As I confess it is my nature's plague
To spy into abuses, and oft my jealousy   147
Shapes faults that are not) – that your wisdom   148
From one that so imperfectly conceits   149
Would take no notice, nor build yourself a trouble   150
Out of his scattering and unsure observance.   151
It were not for your quiet nor your good,
Nor for my manhood, honesty, and wisdom,
To let you know my thoughts.

OTHELLO   What dost thou mean?

IAGO
Good name in man and woman, dear my lord,
Is the immediate jewel of their souls.   156
Who steals my purse steals trash; 'tis something, noth-
   ing;
'Twas mine, 'tis his, and has been slave to thousands.
But he that filches from me my good name
Robs me of that which not enriches him   160
And makes me poor indeed.

139–41 *uncleanly apprehensions . . . lawful* i.e., evil thoughts that do legal
business (*leets*=courts) alongside honorable ideas 147 *jealousy* suspicion
148 *your wisdom* i.e., you 149–50 *From one . . . notice* i.e., wouldn't pay
any attention to me, who unreliably conjectures about things 151 *scattering . . . observance* random and unfounded observations 156 *immediate* inmost

OTHELLO
By heaven, I'll know thy thoughts!

IAGO
You cannot, if my heart were in your hand,
Nor shall not whilst 'tis in my custody.

OTHELLO
Ha!

IAGO O, beware, my lord, of jealousy!
166 It is the green-eyed monster, which doth mock
167 The meat it feeds on. That cuckold lives in bliss
Who, certain of his fate, loves not his wronger;
169 But O, what damnèd minutes tells he o'er
170 Who dotes, yet doubts – suspects, yet soundly loves!

OTHELLO
O misery!

IAGO
Poor and content is rich, and rich enough;
173 But riches fineless is as poor as winter
To him that ever fears he shall be poor.
Good God, the souls of all my tribe defend
From jealousy!

OTHELLO   Why, why is this?
Think'st thou I'd make a life of jealousy,
178 To follow still the changes of the moon
With fresh suspicions? No! To be once in doubt
180 Is once to be resolved. Exchange me for a goat
When I shall turn the business of my soul
182 To such exsufflicate and blowed surmises,
Matching thy inference. 'Tis not to make me jealous
To say my wife is fair, feeds well, loves company,
Is free of speech, sings, plays, and dances;

166–67 *doth mock . . . on* toys with the prey it is about to consume **167–68**
cuckold . . . wronger i.e., a wronged husband doesn't resent an adulterous wife
if he doesn't love her **169** *tells* counts **170** *dotes* loves dotingly; *soundly*
profoundly **173** *fineless* unlimited **178** *still* always **180** *resolved* determined to act **182** *exsufflicate and blowed surmises* (1) spat out and flyblown
(i.e., disgusting) speculations, (2) inflated and blown abroad (rumored) no-
tions

Where virtue is, these are more virtuous.
Nor from mine own weak merits will I draw
The smallest fear or doubt of her revolt,   188
For she had eyes, and chose me. No, Iago;
I'll see before I doubt; when I doubt, prove;   190
And on the proof there is no more but this –
Away at once with love or jealousy!

IAGO
I am glad of this; for now I shall have reason
To show the love and duty that I bear you
With franker spirit. Therefore, as I am bound,   195
Receive it from me. I speak not yet of proof.
Look to your wife; observe her well with Cassio;
Wear your eyes thus, not jealous nor secure.   198
I would not have your free and noble nature,
Out of self-bounty, be abused. Look to't.   200
I know our country disposition well: 201
In Venice they do let God see the pranks
They dare not show their husbands; their best con
    science
Is not to leave't undone, but keep't unknown.

OTHELLO
Dost thou say so?

IAGO
She did deceive her father, marrying you;
And when she seemed to shake and fear your looks,
She loved them most.

OTHELLO   And so she did.

IAGO   Why, go to then!
She that, so young, could give out such a seeming
To seel her father's eyes up close as oak –   210

---

188 *revolt* turning away (i.e., infidelity)   195 *franker* more candid   198 *se-cure* overconfident   200 *self-bounty* i.e., your own natural generosity   201 *our country disposition* i.e., the secret habits of Venetian women (indicated in ll. 202–4)   210 *seel . . . up* shut; *as oak* (referring to the *close* grain of oak – i.e., completely opaque)

He thought 'twas witchcraft – but I am much to blame.
I humbly do beseech you of your pardon
For too much loving you.

OTHELLO   I am bound to thee forever.

IAGO
I see this hath a little dashed your spirits.

OTHELLO
Not a jot, not a jot.

IAGO   I' faith, I fear it has.
I hope you will consider what is spoke
217   Comes from my love. But I do see you're moved.
218   I am to pray you not to strain my speech
To grosser issues nor to larger reach
220   Than to suspicion.

OTHELLO
I will not.

IAGO   Should you do so, my lord,
222   My speech should fall into such vile success
Which my thoughts aimed not. Cassio's my worthy
    friend –
My lord, I see you're moved.

OTHELLO   No, not much moved:
225   I do not think but Desdemona's honest.

IAGO
Long live she so! and long live you to think so!

OTHELLO
And yet, how nature erring from itself –

IAGO
Ay, there's the point! as (to be bold with you)
229   Not to affect many proposed matches
230   Of her own clime, complexion, and degree,
Whereto we see in all things nature tends –

217 *moved* upset 218–19 *strain . . . issues* constrain me to speak of potentially ugly outcomes 222 *vile success* evil result 225 *honest* (primarily
"chaste," but with the suggestion of "honorable") 229–30 *affect . . . degree*
care for proposed husbands from her own background

Foh! one may smell in such a will most rank,   232
Foul disproportions, thoughts unnatural –   233
But pardon me – I do not in position   234
Distinctly speak of her; though I may fear
Her will, recoiling to her better judgment,   236
May fall to match you with her country forms,   237
And happily repent.   238
OTHELLO   Farewell, farewell!
If more thou dost perceive, let me know more.
Set on thy wife to observe. Leave me, Iago.   240
IAGO *[Going]*
My lord, I take my leave.
OTHELLO
Why did I marry? This honest creature doubtless
Sees and knows more, much more, than he unfolds.
IAGO *[Returning]*
My lord, I would I might entreat your honor   244
To scan this thing no farther: leave it to time.   245
Although 'tis fit that Cassio have his place,
For sure he fills it up with great ability,
Yet, if you please to hold him off awhile,
You shall by that perceive him and his means.
Note if your lady strain his entertainment   250
With any strong or vehement importunity;   251
Much will be seen in that. In the meantime
Let me be thought too busy in my fears   253
(As worthy cause I have to fear I am)   254
And hold her free, I do beseech your honor.   255

---

232 *Foh* (expression of disgust); *in such* i.e., in such a headstrong woman;
will sexual appetite (as elsewhere)   233 *disproportions* lack of balance   234
in position i.e., in proposing this characterization   236 *recoiling* yielding
237 *fall . . . forms* i.e., happen to compare you with the Venetian men   238
happily perhaps   240 *Set on* instruct, arrange for   244 *entreat your honor* request you   245 *scan* inspect, consider   250 *strain his entertainment* i.e., insists on discussing his treatment   251 *importunity* begging, pressure   253
too busy i.e., too meddlesome   254 *worthy cause* good reason   255 *hold her
free* consider her innocent

OTHELLO
256   Fear not my government.
IAGO
       I once more take my leave.   *Exit.*
OTHELLO
       This fellow's of exceeding honesty,
259   And knows all qualities, with a learned spirit
260   Of human dealings. If I do prove her haggard,
261   Though that her jesses were my dear heartstrings,
262   I'd whistle her off and let her down the wind
263   To prey at fortune. Haply, for I am black
264   And have not those soft parts of conversation
265   That chamberers have, or for I am declined
       Into the vale of years – yet that's not much –
       She's gone. I am abused, and my relief
       Must be to loathe her. O curse of marriage,
       That we can call these delicate creatures ours,
270   And not their appetites! I had rather be a toad
       And live upon the vapor of a dungeon
       Than keep a corner in the thing I love
273   For others' uses. Yet 'tis the plague of great ones;
274   Prerogatived are they less than the base.
       'Tis destiny unshunnable, like death.
276   Even then this forkèd plague is fated to us
277   When we do quicken. Look where she comes.
            Enter Desdemona and Emilia.
       If she be false, O, then heaven mocks itself!
       I'll not believe't.

---

256 *government* behavior, self-control   259 *qualities* natures; *a learned spirit* an informed understanding   260 *haggard* a wild hawk (beginning a metaphor of Desdemona as an uncontrolled bird)   261 *her jesses* the leather straps for controlling the hawk   262–63 *whistle . . . fortune* i.e., send her away and let her take care of herself   263 *Haply* perhaps   264 *soft . . . conversation* refined manners   265 *chamberers* courtiers   273 *great ones* prominent people   274 *Prerogatived* privileged; *the base* i.e., those of the lower class   276 *forkèd plague* curse of being a cuckold (i.e., with horns on the forehead)   277 *do quicken* are born

DESDEMONA   How now, my dear Othello?
Your dinner, and the generous islanders   280
By you invited, do attend your presence.
OTHELLO
I am to blame.
DESDEMONA   Why do you speak so faintly?
Are you not well?
OTHELLO
I have a pain upon my forehead, here.
DESDEMONA
Faith, that's with watching; 'twill away again.   285
Let me but bind it hard, within this hour
It will be well.   287
OTHELLO   Your napkin is too little;
    [He pushes the handkerchief from him, and it falls
    unnoticed.]
Let it alone. Come, I'll go in with you.   288
DESDEMONA
I am very sorry that you are not well.
                              Exit [with Othello].

EMILIA
I am glad I have found this napkin;   290
This was her first remembrance from the Moor.
My wayward husband hath a hundred times
Wooed me to steal it; but she so loves the token
(For he conjured her she should ever keep it)   294
That she reserves it evermore about her
To kiss and talk to. I'll have the work ta'en out   296
And give't Iago. What he will do with it
Heaven knows, not I;
I nothing but to please his fantasy.   299
    Enter Iago.

---

280 *generous* noble 285 *watching* staying up late (i.e., sleeplessness) 287
napkin handkerchief 288 *Let it alone* i.e., never mind about the headache
294 *conjured her* made her swear (in *conjured* the accent is on the second syllable) 296 *work ta'en out* pattern copied 299 *I nothing . . . fantasy* I do
nothing but please his whims

IAGO

300 How now? What do you here alone?

EMILIA

301 Do not you chide; I have a thing for you.

IAGO

302 You have a thing for me? It is a common thing –

EMILIA   Ha?

IAGO

To have a foolish wife.

EMILIA

O, is that all? What will you give me now
For that same handkerchief?

IAGO   What handkerchief?

EMILIA

What handkerchief!
Why, that the Moor first gave to Desdemona;
That which so often you did bid me steal.

IAGO

310 Hast stol'n it from her?

EMILIA

No, faith; she let it drop by negligence,

312 And to th' advantage, I, being here, took't up.
Look, here 'tis.

IAGO   A good wench! Give it me.

EMILIA

What will you do with't, that you have been so earnest
To have me filch it?

IAGO   Why, what is that to you?

   [Snatches it.]

EMILIA

316 If it be not for some purpose of import,
Give't me again. Poor lady, she'll run mad
When she shall lack it.

---

301 *a thing* an object (but with sexual connotations in the following lines)
302 *common thing* i.e., sexual organ used by everybody   312 *to th' advantage*
opportunely   316 *import* great importance

IAGO
Be not acknown on't; I have use for it.   319
Go, leave me.   *Exit Emilia.*   320
I will in Cassio's lodging lose this napkin
And let him find it. Trifles light as air
Are to the jealous confirmations strong
As proofs of holy writ. This may do something.   324
The Moor already changes with my poison:
Dangerous conceits are in their natures poisons,   326
Which at the first are scarce found to distaste,   327
But with a little act upon the blood
Burn like the mines of sulphur.   329
     Enter Othello.   I did say so.
Look where he comes! Not poppy nor mandragora,   330
Nor all the drowsy syrups of the world,   331
Shall ever med'cine thee to that sweet sleep   332
Which thou owedst yesterday.   333
OTHELLO   Ha! ha! false to me?
IAGO
Why, how now, general? No more of that!
OTHELLO
Avaunt! be gone! Thou hast set me on the rack.   335
I swear 'tis better to be much abused
Than but to know't a little.
IAGO   How now, my lord?
OTHELLO
What sense had I in her stol'n hours of lust?
I saw't not, thought it not, it harmed not me;
I slept the next night well, fed well, was free and merry;   340
I found not Cassio's kisses on her lips.

---

319 *Be . . . on't* don't acknowledge it   324 *proofs of holy writ* biblical truth
326 *conceits* ideas, conceptions   327 *at . . . distaste* initially aren't perceived
to taste bitter   329 *Burn . . . sulphur* i.e., are difficult to extinguish   330
mandragora a narcotic   331 *drowsy* soporific, sleep-inducing   332 *med'cine*
i.e., help by drugs   333 *owedst* owned, enjoyed   335 *Avaunt* away (a command to a devil); *the rack* an instrument of torture   340 *free* carefree

342   He that is robbed, not wanting what is stol'n,
       Let him not know't, and he's not robbed at all.
IAGO
       I am sorry to hear this.
OTHELLO
       I had been happy if the general camp,
346   Pioners and all, had tasted her sweet body,
       So I had nothing known. O, now forever
       Farewell the tranquil mind! farewell content!
349   Farewell the plumèd troops, and the big wars
350   That makes ambition virtue! O, farewell!
       Farewell the neighing steed and the shrill trump,
       The spirit-stirring drum, th' ear-piercing fife,
       The royal banner, and all quality,
354   Pride, pomp, and circumstance of glorious war!
355   And O you mortal engines whose rude throats
       Th' immortal Jove's dread clamors counterfeit,
       Farewell! Othello's occupation's gone!
IAGO
       Is't possible, my lord?
OTHELLO
       Villain, be sure thou prove my love a whore!
360   Be sure of it; give me the ocular proof;
       Or, by the worth of mine eternal soul,
       Thou hadst been better have been born a dog
       Than answer my waked wrath!
IAGO   Is't come to this?
OTHELLO
       Make me to see't; or at the least so prove it
365   That the probation bear no hinge nor loop

---

342 *wanting* missing   346 *Pioners* ditchdiggers, laborers   349 *plumèd troops*
uniformed (*plumèd*=feathered) soldiers; *big wars* mighty conflicts   350
makes ambition virtue i.e., that justify the desire for glory   354 *circumstance*
surrounding pageantry   355 *mortal engines* deadly weapons   355–56
rude . . . counterfeit i.e., noises imitate the thunder (*dread clamors*) of the
heavens   360 *ocular* visible   365 *probation . . . loop* i.e., proof allows no
loophole

To hang a doubt on – or woe upon thy life!

IAGO

My noble lord –

OTHELLO

If thou dost slander her and torture me,
Never pray more; abandon all remorse;
On horror's head horrors accumulate,   370
Do deeds to make heaven weep, all earth amazed;
For nothing canst thou to damnation add
Greater than that.

IAGO   O grace! O heaven forgive me!
Are you a man? Have you a soul or sense? –
God buy you! take mine office. O wretched fool,   375
That lov'st to make thine honesty a vice!   376
O monstrous world! Take note, take note, O world,
To be direct and honest is not safe.
I thank you for this profit, and from hence   379
I'll love no friend, sith love breeds such offense.   380

OTHELLO

Nay, stay. Thou shouldst be honest.   381

IAGO

I should be wise; for honesty's a fool
And loses that it works for.

OTHELLO   By the world,
I think my wife be honest, and think she is not;
I think that thou art just, and think thou art not.   385
I'll have some proof. My name, that was as fresh   386
As Dian's visage, is now begrimed and black   387
As mine own face. If there be cords, or knives,
Poison, or fire, or suffocating streams,

---

375 *God buy you* (abbreviation for "God be with you" – i.e., "good-bye")
376 *That lov'st . . . vice* i.e., who holds so dearly to his honesty as to make it
a liability 379 *profit* beneficial insight 380 *sith* since 381 *shouldst be* (1)
ought to be, (2) i.e., all right, I believe you are honest 385 *just* upright,
honorable 386 *My name* (Q reads "Her name," which is tidier metaphori-
cally) 387 *Dian's visage* the image of Diana, goddess of chastity

390   I'll not endure it. Would I were satisfied!

IAGO

    I see you are eaten up with passion:

392   I do repent me that I put it to you.

    You would be satisfied?

OTHELLO   Would? Nay, and I will.

IAGO

    And may; but how? how satisfied, my lord?

395   Would you, the supervisor, grossly gape on?

396   Behold her topped?

OTHELLO   Death and damnation! O!

IAGO

    It were a tedious difficulty, I think,

398   To bring them to that prospect. Damn them then,

399   If ever mortal eyes do see them bolster

400   More than their own! What then? How then?

    What shall I say? Where's satisfaction?

    It is impossible you should see this,

403   Were they as prime as goats, as hot as monkeys,

404   As salt as wolves in pride, and fools as gross

    As ignorance made drunk. But yet, I say,

406   If imputation and strong circumstances

    Which lead directly to the door of truth

    Will give you satisfaction, you might have't.

OTHELLO

    Give me a living reason she's disloyal.

IAGO

410   I do not like the office.

---

390 *satisfied* absolutely certain (with, in the next four lines, sexual undertones) 392 *put it to you* proposed it 395 *supervisor* spectator, one who
looks down upon 396 *topped* (a visual image for sexual intercourse; "top" is
perhaps a homophone of "tup" [see *tupping* in I.1.88]) 398 *prospect* view,
sight to be seen 399 *bolster* couch (i.e., copulate) 403 *prime* sexually eager
404 *salt as wolves in pride* lecherous as wolves in heat; *gross* indecent, coarse
406 *imputation* charge, accusation; *circumstances* circumstantial evidence
410 *office* task

But sith I am entered in this cause so far,
Pricked to't by foolish honesty and love,   412
I will go on. I lay with Cassio lately,   413
And being troubled with a raging tooth,
I could not sleep.
There are a kind of men so loose of soul
That in their sleeps will mutter their affairs.
One of this kind is Cassio.
In sleep I heard him say "Sweet Desdemona,
Let us be wary, let us hide our loves!"   420
And then, sir, would he gripe and wring my hand,   421
Cry "O sweet creature!" then kiss me hard,
As if he plucked up kisses by the roots
That grew upon my lips, lay his leg o'er my thigh,
And sigh, and kiss, and then cry "Cursèd fate
That gave thee to the Moor."

OTHELLO
O monstrous! monstrous!

IAGO   Nay, this was but his dream.

OTHELLO
But this denoted a foregone conclusion: 428
'Tis a shrewd doubt, though it be but a dream.   429

IAGO
And this may help to thicken other proofs   430
That do demonstrate thinly.

OTHELLO   I'll tear her all to pieces!

IAGO
Nay, yet be wise. Yet we see nothing done;
She may be honest yet. Tell me but this –
Have you not sometimes seen a handkerchief,
Spotted with strawberries, in your wife's hand?

---

412 *Pricked* spurred (but the obscene meaning of "prick" is also audible)
413 *lay* i.e., shared lodgings (sexual undertones are present here as well)
421 *gripe* grip   428 *foregone conclusion* deed already concluded   429 *shrewd
doubt* piercing suspicion   430 *thicken* give substance to

OTHELLO
I gave her such a one; 'twas my first gift.

IAGO
I know not that; but such a handkerchief –
I am sure it was your wife's – did I today
See Cassio wipe his beard with.

OTHELLO   If it be that –

IAGO
440 If it be that, or any that was hers,
It speaks against her with the other proofs.

OTHELLO
442 O, that the slave had forty thousand lives!
One is too poor, too weak for my revenge.
Now do I see 'tis true. Look here, Iago:
All my fond love thus do I blow to heaven.
'Tis gone.
Arise, black vengeance, from the hollow hell!
448 Yield up, O love, thy crown and hearted throne
449 To tyrannous hate! Swell, bosom, with thy fraught,
450 For 'tis of aspics' tongues!

IAGO   Yet be content.

OTHELLO
O, blood, blood, blood!

IAGO
Patience, I say. Your mind may change.

OTHELLO
453 Never, Iago. Like to the Pontic Sea,
Whose icy current and compulsive course
Ne'er feels retiring ebb, but keeps due on
To the Propontic and the Hellespont,
Even so my bloody thoughts, with violent pace,
Shall ne'er look back, ne'er ebb to humble love,

---

442 *slave* i.e., Cassio (the word here means "villain") 448 *hearted throne* i.e.,
love sits royally in the heart 449 *fraught* burden, freight 450 *aspics' tongues*
fangs of asps, venomous snakes 453 *Pontic Sea* Black Sea

Till that a capable and wide revenge   459
Swallow them up.   460
    [He kneels.]   Now, by yond marble heaven,
In the due reverence of a sacred vow
I here engage my words.   462
IAGO   Do not rise yet.
    [Iago kneels.]
Witness, you ever-burning lights above,
You elements that clip us round about,   464
Witness that here Iago doth give up
The execution of his wit, hands, heart   466
To wronged Othello's service! Let him command,
And to obey shall be in me remorse,   468
What bloody business ever.
    [They rise.]
OTHELLO   I greet thy love,
Not with vain thanks but with acceptance bounteous,   470
And will upon the instant put thee to't.   471
Within these three days let me hear thee say
That Cassio's not alive.
IAGO
My friend is dead; 'tis done at your request.
But let her live.
OTHELLO
Damn her, lewd minx! O, damn her! damn her!
Come, go with me apart. I will withdraw
To furnish me with some swift means of death
For the fair devil. Now art thou my lieutenant.
IAGO
I am your own forever.   *Exeunt.*   480

                         *

---

459 *capable* all-embracing, capacious 460 *marble* i.e., shining or perhaps
constant 462 *engage* pledge, guarantee 464 *clip* clasp, embrace 466 *execution* employment, action 468–69 *to . . . ever* i.e., whatever *bloody business*
I'm required to do I'll perform it in pity of Othello 471 *put thee to't* i.e., to
the test

∾ **III.4** *Enter Desdemona, Emilia, and Clown.*

1 DESDEMONA Do you know, sirrah, where Lieutenant
2 Cassio lies?

CLOWN I dare not say he lies anywhere.

DESDEMONA Why, man?

5 CLOWN He's a soldier, and for me to say a soldier lies, 'tis
stabbing.

DESDEMONA Go to. Where lodges he?

CLOWN To tell you where he lodges is to tell you where I
lie.

10 DESDEMONA Can anything be made of this?

11 CLOWN I know not where he lodges; and for me to devise a lodging, and say he lies here or he lies there, were
13 to lie in mine own throat.

14 DESDEMONA Can you inquire him out, and be edified
by report?

16 CLOWN I will catechize the world for him – that is, make
questions, and by them answer.

DESDEMONA Seek him, bid him come hither. Tell him I
19 have moved my lord on his behalf and hope all will be
20 well.

CLOWN To do this is within the compass of man's wit,
and therefore I will attempt the doing it.   *Exit Clown.*

DESDEMONA

Where should I lose the handkerchief, Emilia?

EMILIA

I know not, madam.

DESDEMONA

Believe me, I had rather have lost my purse

III.4 An area outside the castle   1 *sirrah* (a form of "sir" used toward social
inferiors or servants)   2 *lies* lives, stays   5–6 *'tis stabbing* i.e., it puts me in
danger   11–12 *devise* make up   13 *lie . . . throat* lie deeply or foully   14–
15 *edified by report* i.e., instructed (with religious connotations) by what you
hear   16 *catechize* interrogate, search (playing on Desdemona's religious discourse)   19 *moved* solicited

Full of crusadoes. And but my noble Moor   26
Is true of mind, and made of no such baseness
As jealous creatures are, it were enough
To put him to ill thinking.

EMILIA   Is he not jealous?

DESDEMONA
Who? he? I think the sun where he was born   30
Drew all such humors from him.   31

    Enter Othello.

EMILIA   Look where he comes.

DESDEMONA
I will not leave him now till Cassio
Be called to him. – How is't with you, my lord?

OTHELLO
Well, my good lady. *[Aside]* O, hardness to dissemble! –
How do you, Desdemona?

DESDEMONA   Well, my good lord.

OTHELLO
Give me your hand. This hand is moist, my lady.

DESDEMONA
It hath felt no age nor known no sorrow.

OTHELLO
This argues fruitfulness and liberal heart.   38
Hot, hot, and moist. This hand of yours requires
A sequester from liberty; fasting and prayer,   40
Much castigation, exercise devout;   41
For here's a young and sweating devil here
That commonly rebels. 'Tis a good hand,
A frank one.   44

DESDEMONA   You may, indeed, say so;
For 'twas that hand that gave away my heart.

---

26 *crusadoes* gold coins (with a figure of the cross, *crux*); *And but* i.e., if it were not that 31 *humors* bodily fluids governing temperament 38 *argues . . . heart* signifies fecundity, sexual abundance, and licentiousness 40 *sequester* separation 41 *castigation* holy correction 44 *frank* free, open (with sexual sense)

OTHELLO
46 A liberal hand! The hearts of old gave hands,
But our new heraldry is hands, not hearts.

DESDEMONA
I cannot speak of this. Come now, your promise!

OTHELLO
49 What promise, chuck?

DESDEMONA
50 I have sent to bid Cassio come speak with you.

OTHELLO
51 I have a salt and sorry rheum offends me.
Lend me thy handkerchief.

DESDEMONA   Here, my lord.

OTHELLO
That which I gave you.

DESDEMONA   I have it not about me.

OTHELLO
Not?

DESDEMONA   No, faith, my lord.

OTHELLO   That's a fault.
That handkerchief
56 Did an Egyptian to my mother give.
57 She was a charmer, and could almost read
The thoughts of people. She told her, while she kept it,
59 'Twould make her amiable and subdue my father
60 Entirely to her love; but if she lost it
Or made a gift of it, my father's eye
Should hold her loathèd, and his spirits should hunt
63 After new fancies. She, dying, gave it me,
And bid me, when my fate would have me wived,
65 To give it her. I did so; and take heed on't;

46–47 *The hearts ... hearts* i.e., in better days people pledged their hearts with their hands, but now, in modern symbols of courtship (*heraldry*), the two no longer go together **49** *chuck* (a term of affection; cf. *wretch*, III.3.90) **51** *salt and sorry rheum* painful running cold **56** *Egyptian* (probably "gypsy") **57** *charmer* sorceress **59** *amiable* desirable **63** *fancies* loves, attractions **65** *her* i.e., the intended bride

Make it a darling like your precious eye.   66
To lose't or give't away were such perdition   67
As nothing else could match.
DESDEMONA   Is't possible?
OTHELLO
'Tis true. There's magic in the web of it.   69
A sibyl that had numbered in the world   70
The sun to course two hundred compasses,   71
In her prophetic fury sewed the work;
The worms were hallowed that did breed the silk;
And it was dyed in mummy which the skillful   74
Conserved of maidens' hearts.
DESDEMONA   I' faith? Is't true?
OTHELLO
Most veritable. Therefore look to't well.
DESDEMONA
Then would to God that I had never seen't!
OTHELLO   Ha! Wherefore?
DESDEMONA
Why do you speak so startingly and rash?   79
OTHELLO
Is't lost? Is't gone? Speak, is't out o' th' way?   80
DESDEMONA   Heaven bless us!
OTHELLO   Say you?
DESDEMONA
It is not lost. But what an if it were?   83
OTHELLO   How?
DESDEMONA
I say it is not lost.
OTHELLO   Fetch't, let me see't!
DESDEMONA
Why, so I can, but I will not now.

---

66 *darling* beloved thing; *eye* (early modern slang for the vagina, a sense that may pertain here) 67 *perdition* loss, disaster 69 *web* fabric 70 *sibyl* prophetess 71 *sun ... compasses* i.e., two hundred years 74–75 *mummy ... hearts* a drug distilled (*Conserved*) from mummified bodies, here from *maidens' hearts* 79 *startingly* by starts, fitfully 83 *an if* if

87   This is a trick to put me from my suit:
        Pray you let Cassio be received again.
OTHELLO
89   Fetch me the handkerchief! My mind misgives.
DESDEMONA
90   Come, come!
91   You'll never meet a more sufficient man.
OTHELLO
92   The handkerchief!
DESDEMONA   A man that all his time
        Hath founded his good fortunes on your love,
        Shared dangers with you –
OTHELLO
        The handkerchief!
DESDEMONA
        I' faith, you are to blame.
OTHELLO   Zounds!   *Exit Othello.*
EMILIA   Is not this man jealous?
DESDEMONA
        I ne'er saw this before.
100   Sure there's some wonder in this handkerchief;
        I am most unhappy in the loss of it.
EMILIA
102   'Tis not a year or two shows us a man.
103   They are all but stomachs, and we all but food;
        They eat us hungerly, and when they are full,
        They belch us.
            Enter Iago and Cassio.
                    Look you – Cassio and my husband!
IAGO
        There is no other way; 'tis she must do't.
107   And lo the happiness! Go and importune her.

---

87 *put me from* distract me from   89 *misgives* feels doubt or regret   91 *sufficient* thoroughly capable   92 *all his time* throughout his career   102 *'Tis
not . . . man* i.e., it takes a long time to know a man's real self (or perhaps
"good men don't come along very often")   103 *all but* nothing except   107
lo the happiness i.e., and what luck that she is here; *importune* ask

DESDEMONA
     How now, good Cassio? What's the news with you?
CASSIO
     Madam, my former suit. I do beseech you
     That by your virtuous means I may again   *110*
     Exist, and be a member of his love
     Whom I with all the office of my heart   112
     Entirely honor. I would not be delayed.
     If my offense be of such mortal kind   114
     That nor my service past, nor present sorrows,
     Nor purposed merit in futurity,
     Can ransom me into his love again,
     But to know so must be my benefit.   118
     So shall I clothe me in a forced content,   119
     And shut myself up in some other course,   120
     To fortune's alms.   121
DESDEMONA   Alas, thrice-gentle Cassio!
     My advocation is not now in tune.   122
     My lord is not my lord; nor should I know him,
     Were he in favor as in humor altered.   124
     So help me every spirit sanctified
     As I have spoken for you all my best
     And stood within the blank of his displeasure   12*7*
     For my free speech! You must awhile be patient.
     What I can do I will; and more I will
     Than for myself I dare. Let that suffice you.   *130*
IAGO
     Is my lord angry?
EMILIA   He went hence but now,
     And certainly in strange unquietness.

---

112 *office* devoted service   114 *mortal* i.e., hopeless   118 *But . . . benefit*
merely to know it will be helpful   119 *So* in that case; *forced content* necessary contentment (i.e., being resigned to it)   120 *shut myself up in* limit myself to   121 *fortune's alms* the best I can get from fortune   122 *advocation*
advocacy   124 *favor* appearance; *humor* mood, temperament   127 *blank*
center of a target (also known as the "white")

IAGO
Can he be angry? I have seen the cannon
When it hath blown his ranks into the air
And, like the devil, from his very arm
Puffed his own brother – and is he angry?
137 Something of moment then. I will go meet him.
There's matter in't indeed if he be angry.

DESDEMONA
139 I prithee do so.   *Exit [Iago].*
Something sure of state,
140 Either from Venice or some unhatched practice
Made demonstrable here in Cyprus to him,
142 Hath puddled his clear spirit; and in such cases
143 Men's natures wrangle with inferior things,
Though great ones are their object. 'Tis even so;
145 For let our finger ache, and it endues
Our other, healthful members even to a sense
Of pain. Nay, we must think men are not gods,
148 Nor of them look for such observancy
149 As fits the bridal. Beshrew me much, Emilia,
150 I was, unhandsome warrior as I am,
151 Arraigning his unkindness with my soul;
152 But now I find I had suborned the witness,
And he's indicted falsely.

EMILIA
Pray heaven it be state matters, as you think,
155 And no conception nor no jealous toy
Concerning you.

---

137 *of moment* momentous, significant   139 *of state* having to do with poli-
tics   140 *unhatched practice* still-hidden plot   142 *puddled* disturbed, mud-
died   143–44 *wrangle . . . object* i.e., bicker over or debate about trivia when
they are really concerned with major topics   145 *endues* introduces   148–
49 *observancy . . . bridal* i.e., attentiveness expected on the wedding day
149 *Beshrew me* (a mild oath, the equivalent of "I'll be darned")   150 *unhandsome warrior* poor soldier   151 *Arraigning his unkindness* indicting his
abnormal (not according to kind) behavior toward me   152 *suborned the
witness* bribed the witness (i.e., herself) to lie   155 *conception* fantasy, wild
idea; *toy* whim, foolish fancy

DESDEMONA
  Alas the day! I never gave him cause.   157
EMILIA
  But jealous souls will not be answered so;
  They are not ever jealous for the cause,
  But jealous for they're jealous. It is a monster   160
  Begot upon itself, born on itself.   161
DESDEMONA
  Heaven keep the monster from Othello's mind!
EMILIA   Lady, amen.
DESDEMONA
  I will go seek him. Cassio, walk hereabout:
  If I do find him fit, I'll move your suit   165
  And seek to effect it to my uttermost.
CASSIO
  I humbly thank your ladyship.
                        Exit [Desdemona with Emilia].
      Enter Bianca.
BIANCA
  Save you, friend Cassio!   168
CASSIO   What make you from home?
  How is't with you, my most fair Bianca?
  I' faith, sweet love, I was coming to your house.   *170*
BIANCA
  And I was going to your lodging, Cassio.
  What, keep a week away? seven days and nights?
  Eightscore eight hours? and lovers' absent hours,   173
  More tedious than the dial eightscore times?   174
  O weary reck'ning!
CASSIO   Pardon me, Bianca:
  I have this while with leaden thoughts been pressed,
  But I shall in a more continuate time   177

---

157 *Alas the day* (conventional lament – "What a shame")   160 *for* because
161 *Begot upon itself* self-engendered   165 *fit* receptive, fit to listen   168
Save you God save you; *What make you from* what are you doing away from
173 *Eightscore eight hours* one hundred sixty-eight hours, the number in a
week   174 *dial* clock   177 *more continuate* less interrupted, less fretful

178   Strike off this score of absence. Sweet Bianca,
      [Gives her Desdemona's handkerchief.]
179   Take me this work out.
      BIANCA   O Cassio, whence came this?
180   This is some token from a newer friend.
181   To the felt absence now I feel a cause.
      Is't come to this? Well, well.
      CASSIO   Go to, woman!
      Throw your vile guesses in the devil's teeth,
      From whence you have them. You are jealous now
      That this is from some mistress, some remembrance.
      No, by my faith, Bianca.
      BIANCA   Why, whose is it?
      CASSIO
      I know not, neither; I found it in my chamber.
188   I like the work well; ere it be demanded,
      As like enough it will, I would have it copied.
190   Take it and do't, and leave me for this time.
      BIANCA
      Leave you? Wherefore?
      CASSIO
      I do attend here on the general
193   And think it no addition, nor my wish,
      To have him see me womaned.
      BIANCA   Why, I pray you?
      CASSIO
      Not that I love you not.
      BIANCA   But that you do not love me!
196   I pray you bring me on the way a little,
      And say if I shall see you soon at night.
      CASSIO
      'Tis but a little way that I can bring you,

---

178 *Strike off this score* pay this bill   179 *Take . . . out* copy this embroidery
(*work*=needlework) for me   181 *To . . . cause* i.e., I can now explain your
absence from me   188 *ere it be demanded* i.e., before somebody claims it
193 *no addition* no bonus – i.e., not beneficial to my standing   196 *bring
me* go along with me

For I attend here, but I'll see you soon.   199
BIANCA
'Tis very good. I must be circumstanced.   200

Exeunt omnes.

*

∽ **IV.1** *Enter Othello and Iago.*

IAGO
Will you think so?
OTHELLO   Think so, Iago?
IAGO   What,
To kiss in private?
OTHELLO   An unauthorized kiss.
IAGO
Or to be naked with her friend in bed
An hour or more, not meaning any harm?
OTHELLO
Naked in bed, Iago, and not mean harm?
It is hypocrisy against the devil.   6
They that mean virtuously, and yet do so,   7
The devil their virtue tempts, and they tempt heaven.
IAGO
If they do nothing, 'tis a venial slip.   9
But if I give my wife a handkerchief –   10
OTHELLO
What then?
IAGO
Why, then 'tis hers, my lord, and being hers,
She may, I think, bestow't on any man.
OTHELLO
She is protectress of her honor too;

---

199 *attend* am waiting   200 *circumstanced* governed by things as they are;
s.d. *omnes* all
   IV.1 An area outside Othello's quarters   6 *hypocrisy against the devil* i.e.,
apparent evil concealing good (ironic)   7 *yet do so* i.e., still allow themselves
to be naked in bed   9 *venial slip* minor sin

May she give that?

IAGO

Her honor is an essence that's not seen;

17   They have it very oft that have it not.

But for the handkerchief –

OTHELLO

By heaven, I would most gladly have forgot it!

20   Thou said'st – O, it comes o'er my memory

21   As doth the raven o'er the infectious house,

22   Boding to all! – he had my handkerchief.

IAGO

Ay, what of that?

OTHELLO   That's not so good now.

IAGO   What

If I had said I had seen him do you wrong?

25   Or heard him say – as knaves be such abroad

26   Who having, by their own importunate suit,

Or voluntary dotage of some mistress,

Convincèd or supplied them, cannot choose

But they must blab –

OTHELLO   Hath he said anything?

IAGO

30   He hath, my lord; but be you well assured,

No more than he'll unswear.

OTHELLO   What hath he said?

IAGO

Faith, that he did – I know not what he did.

OTHELLO   What? what?

IAGO

34   Lie –

OTHELLO   With her?

IAGO   With her, on her; what you will.

---

17 *They . . . not* many people who seem to have it in fact do not   **21** *infectious* plague-ridden   **22** *Boding* prophesying (ill)   **25** *knaves . . . abroad* there are men around   **26–28** *by . . . them* i.e., achieved satisfaction either by insistent wooing or by the irresistible attraction they exert over a woman   **34** *what you will* (a conventional phrase – "as you like it" – ending with the sexually charged *will*)

OTHELLO   Lie with her? lie on her? – We say lie on her
when they belie her. – Lie with her! Zounds, that's ful-   36
some. – Handkerchief – confessions – handkerchief! –
To confess, and be hanged for his labor – first to be   38
hanged, and then to confess! I tremble at it. Nature   39
would not invest herself in such shadowing passion   40
without some instruction. It is not words that shakes   41
me thus. – Pish! Noses, ears, and lips? Is't possible? –
Confess? – Handkerchief? – O devil!
    Falls in a trance.
IAGO   Work on,
My medicine works! Thus credulous fools are caught,   45
And many worthy and chaste dames even thus,
All guiltless, meet reproach. – What, ho! my lord!
My lord, I say! Othello!
    Enter Cassio.   How now, Cassio?
CASSIO
What's the matter?
IAGO
My lord is fall'n into an epilepsy.   50
This is his second fit; he had one yesterday.
CASSIO
Rub him about the temples.
IAGO   No, forbear.
The lethargy must have his quiet course.   53
If not, he foams at mouth, and by and by
Breaks out to savage madness. Look, he stirs.
Do you withdraw yourself a little while.
He will recover straight. When he is gone,
I would on great occasion speak with you.   58
                                        [Exit Cassio.]

---

36 *belie* slander   36–37 *fulsome* foul   38–39 *To confess . . . confess* ("To confess and be hanged" was a proverbial phrase; Othello uses and then inverts it)
39–41 *Nature . . . instruction* nature wouldn't permit such strong emotion
that produces these images (*shadowing passion*) without a basis for it   41
words i.e., words only   45 *medicine* (1) poison, (2) medicine   53 *lethargy*
state of unconsciousness; *his* its   58 *great occasion* significant matter

    How is it, general? Have you not hurt your head?
OTHELLO
60   Dost thou mock me?
IAGO   I mock you not, by heaven.
    Would you would bear your fortune like a man!
OTHELLO
    A hornèd man's a monster and a beast.
IAGO
    There's many a beast then in a populous city,
64   And many a civil monster.
OTHELLO
    Did he confess it?
IAGO   Good sir, be a man.
66   Think every bearded fellow that's but yoked
67   May draw with you. There's millions now alive
68   That nightly lie in those unproper beds
69   Which they dare swear peculiar: your case is better.
70   O, 'tis the spite of hell, the fiend's arch-mock,
71   To lip a wanton in a secure couch,
72   And to suppose her chaste! No, let me know;
    And knowing what I am, I know what she shall be.
OTHELLO
    O, thou art wise! 'Tis certain.
IAGO   Stand you awhile apart;
75   Confine yourself but in a patient list.
    Whilst you were here, o'erwhelmèd with your grief –
    A passion most unsuiting such a man –
    Cassio came hither. I shifted him away

---

60 *mock me* (Othello reads Iago's *hurt your head,* l. 59, as a joke about cuck-oldry, wearing horns; also see l. 62) **64** *civil* civilized, domesticated **66** *yoked* married (but also yoked like an ox; the image introduces a series of puns on marriage, yoking, and horned beasts) **67** *draw* (1) compare, (2) pull a cart **68** *unproper* not exclusively their own **69** *peculiar* theirs alone; *your . . . better* i.e., at least you know **71** *lip . . . couch* kiss a whore in an apparently untainted bed (*secure couch*) **72–73** *No . . . be* i.e., I'd rather know that I'm a cuckold, and then I can take action against her **75** *Confine . . . list* stay within the limits of self-control

And laid good 'scuses upon your ecstasy;   79
Bade him anon return, and here speak with me;   80
The which he promised. Do but encave yourself   81
And mark the fleers, the gibes, and notable scorns   82
That dwell in every region of his face;
For I will make him tell the tale anew –
Where, how, how oft, how long ago, and when
He hath, and is again to cope your wife.   86
I say, but mark his gesture. Marry, patience!
Or I shall say you're all in all in spleen,   88
And nothing of a man.
OTHELLO   Dost thou hear, Iago?
I will be found most cunning in my patience;   90
But – dost thou hear? – most bloody.
IAGO   That's not amiss;
But yet keep time in all. Will you withdraw?
    [Othello retires.]
Now will I question Cassio of Bianca,
A huswife that by selling her desires   94
Buys herself bread and cloth. It is a creature
That dotes on Cassio, as 'tis the strumpet's plague
To beguile many and be beguiled by one.   97
He, when he hears of her, cannot restrain
From the excess of laughter. Here he comes.
    Enter Cassio.
As he shall smile, Othello shall go mad,   100
And his unbookish jealousy must conster   101
Poor Cassio's smiles, gestures, and light behaviors   102
Quite in the wrong. How do you now, lieutenant?

---

79 *ecstasy* trance (*ec-stasy* = out of one's natural state)   **80** *anon* shortly   **81**
encave conceal   **82** *fleers* sneers   **86** *cope* get together with (in both senses)
88 *all in all in spleen* flooded entirely with choler (the humor of the *spleen*,
seat of passionate anger)   **94** *huswife* (not only "hussy" or "prostitute" but
also "a woman who manages her household with skill and thrift, a domestic
economist" [*OED*]; see the dispute with Emilia, V.1.123–24)   **97** *beguile*
enchant, deceive   **101** *unbookish* naive; *conster* construe, interpret   **102**
light cheerful, casual

CASSIO
104 The worser that you give me the addition
105 Whose want even kills me.
IAGO
Ply Desdemona well, and you are sure on't.
Now, if this suit lay in Bianca's power,
108 How quickly should you speed!
CASSIO   Alas, poor caitiff!
OTHELLO
Look how he laughs already!
IAGO
110 I never knew a woman love man so.
CASSIO
111 Alas, poor rogue! I think, i' faith, she loves me.
OTHELLO
112 Now he denies it faintly, and laughs it out.
IAGO
Do you hear, Cassio?
OTHELLO   Now he importunes him
114 To tell it o'er. Go to! Well said, well said!
IAGO
She gives it out that you shall marry her.
Do you intend it?
CASSIO   Ha, ha, ha!
OTHELLO
118 Do ye triumph, Roman? Do you triumph?
119 CASSIO   I marry? What, a customer? Prithee bear some
120 charity to my wit; do not think it so unwholesome. Ha,
ha, ha!
OTHELLO   So, so, so, so! They laugh that wins!
IAGO
123 Faith, the cry goes that you marry her.

---

104 *addition* title, rank   105 *want* lack   108 *speed* succeed; *caitiff* wretch
111 *rogue* rascal (a term of endearment)   112 *denies it faintly* i.e., doesn't
strenuously object to the suggestion   114 *Well said* i.e., well done, good
work   118 *Roman* i.e., victor, associated with *triumph*   119 *customer* prostitute, one who sells herself   123 *cry* rumor

CASSIO   Prithee say true.

IAGO   I am a very villain else.

OTHELLO   Have you scored me? Well.   126

CASSIO   This is the monkey's own giving out. She is per-
suaded I will marry her out of her own love and flattery,
not out of my promise.

OTHELLO   Iago beckons me; now he begins the story.   130

CASSIO   She was here even now; she haunts me in every
place. I was the other day talking on the sea bank with
certain Venetians, and thither comes the bauble, and   133
falls me thus about my neck –

OTHELLO   Crying "O dear Cassio!" as it were. His gesture imports it.

CASSIO   So hangs, and lolls, and weeps upon me; so
shakes and pulls me! Ha, ha, ha!

OTHELLO   Now he tells how she plucked him to my
chamber. O, I see that nose of yours, but not that dog I   140
shall throw it to.

CASSIO   Well, I must leave her company.

Enter Bianca

IAGO   Before me! Look where she comes.

CASSIO   'Tis such another fitchew! marry, a perfumed   144
one. What do you mean by this haunting of me?

BIANCA   Let the devil and his dam haunt you! What did   146
you mean by that same handkerchief you gave me even
now? I was a fine fool to take it. I must take out the
work? A likely piece of work that you should find it in   149
your chamber and know not who left it there! This is   150
some minx's token, and I must take out the work?   151

---

126 *scored* beaten, scored off   130 *beckons* signals   133 *bauble* playtoy
140–41 *I . . . to* (Othello imagines dismembering Cassio; *nose* could be a euphemism for "penis")   144 *such another fitchew* just such a (notoriously
lecherous) polecat (i.e., prostitute) as we were talking of; *perfumed* (alluding
to the odor of the polecat)   146 *dam* mother ("devil's dam" was a proverbial
phrase)   149 *likely piece of work* likely story, fiction   151 *minx's token* present from a whore

152   There! Give it your hobbyhorse. Wheresoever you had
it, I'll take out no work on't.

CASSIO   How now, my sweet Bianca? How now? how
now?

156 OTHELLO   By heaven, that should be my handkerchief!

BIANCA   If you'll come to supper tonight, you may; if
158   you will not, come when you are next prepared for.

                                               Exit.

IAGO   After her, after her!

160 CASSIO   Faith, I must; she'll rail in the streets else.

IAGO   Will you sup there?

CASSIO   Faith, I intend so.

IAGO   Well, I may chance to see you; for I would very
164   fain speak with you.

CASSIO   Prithee come. Will you?

IAGO   Go to! say no more.   *[Exit Cassio.]*

OTHELLO   *[Comes forward.]* How shall I murder him, Iago?

168 IAGO   Did you perceive how he laughed at his vice?

OTHELLO   O Iago!

170 IAGO   And did you see the handkerchief?

OTHELLO   Was that mine?

172 IAGO   Yours, by this hand! And to see how he prizes the
foolish woman your wife! She gave it him, and he hath
given it his whore.

OTHELLO   I would have him nine years a-killing! – A fine
woman! a fair woman! a sweet woman!

IAGO   Nay, you must forget that.

OTHELLO   Ay, let her rot, and perish, and be damned
tonight, for she shall not live. No, my heart is turned to
180   stone; I strike it, and it hurts my hand. O, the world
hath not a sweeter creature! She might lie by an em-
182   peror's side and command him tasks.

----

152 *your hobbyhorse* i.e., to whatever slut gave it to you 156 *should* i.e.,
must 158 *next prepared for* i.e., the next time you are invited (which will be
never) 160 *rail* complain shrewishly 164 *fain* eagerly 168 *vice* i.e., his
weakness for women 172 *by this hand* i.e., I swear by this hand; *prizes* values 182 *command him tasks* give him orders

IAGO   Nay, that's not your way.

OTHELLO   Hang her! I do but say what she is. So delicate with her needle! an admirable musician! O, she will sing the savageness out of a bear! Of so high and plenteous wit and invention –   187

IAGO   She's the worse for all this.

OTHELLO   O, a thousand, a thousand times! And then, of so gentle a condition!   190

IAGO   Ay, too gentle.

OTHELLO   Nay, that's certain. But yet the pity of it, Iago! O Iago, the pity of it, Iago!

IAGO   If you are so fond over her iniquity, give her patent   194
to offend; for if it touch not you, it comes near nobody.   195

OTHELLO   I will chop her into messes! Cuckold me!   196

IAGO   O, 'tis foul in her.

OTHELLO   With mine officer!

IAGO   That's fouler.

OTHELLO   Get me some poison, Iago, this night. I'll not   *200*
expostulate with her, lest her body and beauty unpro   *201*
vide my mind again. This night, Iago!

IAGO   Do it not with poison. Strangle her in her bed, even the bed she hath contaminated.

OTHELLO   Good, good! The justice of it pleases. Very good!

IAGO   And for Cassio, let me be his undertaker: you shall   207
hear more by midnight.

OTHELLO
Excellent good!
   [A trumpet.] What trumpet is that same?

---

187 *invention* imagination   190 *gentle a condition* (1) pleasant temperament, (2) genteel social position   194 *patent* license   195 *touch not you* doesn't concern you   196 *messes* pieces of food suitable for meals (i.e., "to bits")   201 *expostulate* converse, dispute   201–2 *unprovide my mind* i.e., change my determination   207 *his undertaker* (1) one who acts as security for another (i.e., "I'll take care of him"), (2) one who takes up a challenge (probably not yet in the modern sense of funeral director)

IAGO
210   I warrant something from Venice.
        Enter Lodovico, Desdemona, and Attendants.
                                        'Tis Lodovico.
        This comes from the duke. See, your wife's with him.
LODOVICO
212   God save you, worthy general!
OTHELLO   With all my heart, sir.
LODOVICO
        The duke and the senators of Venice greet you.
        [Gives him a letter.]
OTHELLO
214   I kiss the instrument of their pleasures.
        [Opens the letter and reads.]
DESDEMONA
        And what's the news, good cousin Lodovico?
IAGO
        I am very glad to see you, signor.
        Welcome to Cyprus.
LODOVICO
        I thank you. How does Lieutenant Cassio?
IAGO   Lives, sir.
DESDEMONA
        Cousin, there's fall'n between him and my lord
220   An unkind breach; but you shall make all well.
OTHELLO   Are you sure of that?
DESDEMONA   My lord?
OTHELLO   *[Reads.]* "This fail you not to do, as you will –"
LODOVICO
        He did not call; he's busy in the paper.
        Is there division 'twixt my lord and Cassio?
DESDEMONA
        A most unhappy one. I would do much

---

210 *warrant* feel sure   212 *With all my heart* (a reciprocal compliment to
Lodovico's greeting)   214 *instrument* i.e., letter

T' atone them, for the love I bear to Cassio.   227
OTHELLO
  Fire and brimstone!
DESDEMONA   My lord?
OTHELLO   Are you wise?
DESDEMONA
  What, is he angry?
LODOVICO   May be the letter moved him;
  For, as I think, they do command him home,   230
  Deputing Cassio in his government.   231
DESDEMONA
  By my troth, I am glad on't.
OTHELLO   Indeed?
DESDEMONA   My lord?
OTHELLO
  I am glad to see you mad.   233
DESDEMONA   Why, sweet Othello?
OTHELLO   Devil!
  [Strikes her.]
DESDEMONA   I have not deserved this.
LODOVICO
  My lord, this would not be believed in Venice,
  Though I should swear I saw't. 'Tis very much.   237
  Make her amends; she weeps.
OTHELLO   O devil, devil!
  If that the earth could teem with woman's tears,   239
  Each drop she falls would prove a crocodile.   240
  Out of my sight!
DESDEMONA   I will not stay to offend you.   *[Going]*
LODOVICO
  Truly, an obedient lady,

---

227 *atone them* reconcile them, make them united ("at one")   231 *Deputing . . . government* i.e., giving Othello's office to Cassio   233 *glad . . . mad* i.e., I am pleased that you are foolish enough to rejoice in this news (with a possible pun on "maid")   237 *very much* i.e., too much, unbelievable   239 *teem* breed   240 *crocodile* (notorious for weeping false tears as a means of ensnaring human victims)

I do beseech your lordship call her back.

OTHELLO
Mistress!

DESDEMONA My lord?

OTHELLO What would you with her, sir?

LODOVICO
Who? I, my lord?

OTHELLO
246 Ay! You did wish that I would make her turn.
Sir, she can turn, and turn, and yet go on
And turn again; and she can weep, sir, weep;
249 And she's obedient; as you say, obedient,
250 Very obedient. – Proceed you in your tears. –
251 Concerning this, sir – O well-painted passion! –
I am commanded home. – Get you away;
I'll send for you anon. – Sir, I obey the mandate
And will return to Venice. – Hence, avaunt!

[Exit Desdemona.]

Cassio shall have my place. And, sir, tonight
I do entreat that we may sup together.
257 You are welcome, sir, to Cyprus. – Goats and monkeys!

Exit.

LODOVICO
Is this the noble Moor whom our full Senate
Call all in all sufficient? Is this the nature
260 Whom passion could not shake? whose solid virtue
The shot of accident nor dart of chance
Could neither graze nor pierce?

IAGO He is much changed.

---

246 *turn* turn back (but with a multiple pun, repeated in the following lines, on *turn* as [1] change indiscriminately, [2] pursue sexual encounters, as in the modern "turn tricks") 249 *obedient* (Othello twists Lodovico's use of the word in l. 242 to suggest "easy," "yielding" – i.e., sexually pliant) 251 *well-painted passion* artfully counterfeited sorrow 257 *Goats and monkeys* (apparently a muttered reference to the lecherous animals mentioned in III.3.403–4)

LODOVICO
  Are his wits safe? Is he not light of brain?   263
IAGO
  He's that he is; I may not breathe my censure.   264
  What he might be – if what he might he is not –   265
  I would to heaven he were!
LODOVICO   What, strike his wife?
IAGO
  Faith, that was not so well; yet would I knew
  That stroke would prove the worst!   268
LODOVICO   Is it his use?
  Or did the letters work upon his blood
  And new create his fault?   270
IAGO   Alas, alas!
  It is not honesty in me to speak
  What I have seen and known. You shall observe him,
  And his own courses will denote him so   273
  That I may save my speech. Do but go after
  And mark how he continues.
LODOVICO
  I am sorry that I am deceived in him.   *Exeunt.*

                          *

  ∾ **IV.2** *Enter Othello and Emilia.*

OTHELLO
  You have seen nothing then?
EMILIA
  Nor ever heard, nor ever did suspect.
OTHELLO
  Yes, you have seen Cassio and she together.

---

263 *safe* sound, normal   264 *censure* opinion, judgment   **265–66** *What . . .*
were i.e., if he's not insane, then he ought to be (to explain this behavior)
268 *use* custom   **273** *courses* modes of action
    IV.2 A room in the castle

EMILIA
But then I saw no harm, and then I heard
Each syllable that breath made up between them.
OTHELLO
What, did they never whisper?
EMILIA   Never, my lord.
OTHELLO
Nor send you out o' th' way?
EMILIA   Never.
OTHELLO
To fetch her fan, her gloves, her mask, nor nothing?
10   EMILIA   Never, my lord.
OTHELLO   That's strange.
EMILIA
12   I durst, my lord, to wager she is honest,
Lay down my soul at stake. If you think other,
14   Remove your thought; it doth abuse your bosom.
If any wretch have put this in your head,
16   Let heaven requite it with the serpent's curse!
For if she be not honest, chaste, and true,
There's no man happy; the purest of their wives
Is foul as slander.
OTHELLO   Bid her come hither. Go. *Exit Emilia.*
20   She says enough; yet she's a simple bawd
21   That cannot say as much. This is a subtle whore,
22   A closet lock and key of villainous secrets;
And yet she'll kneel and pray; I have seen her do't.
        Enter Desdemona and Emilia.
DESDEMONA
24   My lord, what is your will?

---

12 *durst* would dare   14 *abuse your bosom* deceive your heart   16 *with the serpent's curse* i.e., by making him move eternally on the belly (see Genesis 3:14)   20 *simple bawd* foolish pimp (Othello figures Emilia as a brothel keeper protecting her merchandise, the whore)   21 *This* i.e., Desdemona   22 *closet lock and key* i.e., a closed cabinet   24 *what is your will* (Desdemona's words resemble the greeting of a courtesan seeking to please her client; see note to *wills* at I.3.321)

OTHELLO   Pray you, chuck, come hither.
DESDEMONA
  What is your pleasure?
OTHELLO   Let me see your eyes.
  Look in my face.
DESDEMONA   What horrible fancy's this?
OTHELLO   [To Emilia]
  Some of your function, mistress.   27
  Leave procreants alone and shut the door;   28
  Cough or cry hem if anybody come.
  Your mystery, your mystery! Nay, dispatch!   30
                                    Exit Emilia.

DESDEMONA
  Upon my knee, what doth your speech import?
  I understand a fury in your words,
  But not the words.
OTHELLO
  Why, what art thou?
DESDEMONA   Your wife, my lord, your true
  And loyal wife.
OTHELLO   Come, swear it, damn thyself;
  Lest, being like one of heaven, the devils themselves   36
  Should fear to seize thee. Therefore be double-
    damned –
  Swear thou art honest.   38
DESDEMONA   Heaven doth truly know it.
OTHELLO
  Heaven truly knows that thou art false as hell.
DESDEMONA
  To whom, my lord? With whom? How am I false?   40
OTHELLO
  Ah, Desdemon! away! away! away!

---

27 *Some . . . mistress* i.e., do your job by leaving us alone and watching the door   28 *procreants* procreators, copulators   30 *mystery* trade   36 *being . . . heaven* looking like an angel as you do   38 *honest* chaste

DESDEMONA
Alas the heavy day! Why do you weep?
Am I the motive of these tears, my lord?
If haply you my father do suspect
45   An instrument of this your calling back,
Lay not your blame on me. If you have lost him,
I have lost him too.

OTHELLO   Had it pleased heaven
To try me with affliction, had they rained
All kinds of sores and shames on my bare head,
50   Steeped me in poverty to the very lips,
Given to captivity me and my utmost hopes,
I should have found in some place of my soul
A drop of patience. But, alas, to make me
54   The fixèd figure for the time of scorn
To point his slow and moving finger at!
Yet could I bear that too; well, very well.
57   But there where I have garnered up my heart,
Where either I must live or bear no life,
59   The fountain from the which my current runs
60   Or else dries up – to be discarded thence,
61   Or keep it as a cistern for foul toads
62   To knot and gender in – turn thy complexion there,
Patience, thou young and rose-lipped cherubin!
Ay, here look grim as hell!

DESDEMONA
I hope my noble lord esteems me honest.

OTHELLO
66   O, ay, as summer flies are in the shambles,

---

45 *An instrument* a means   54–55 *fixèd . . . at* object of ridicule for a scornful age, which is figured as a clock; the dial moves without appearing to (*slow
and moving finger*)   57 *garnered up* stored, put for safekeeping   59 *fountain*
spring   61 *cistern* cesspool, filthy sink   62 *knot and gender* copulate, repro-
duce   62–64 *turn . . . hell* i.e., if you, Patience, look on that, your cherubic
appearance will become as *grim as hell*   66 *shambles* slaughterhouse

That quicken even with blowing. O thou weed,   67
Who art so lovely fair, and smell'st so sweet,
That the sense aches at thee, would thou hadst never
    been born!

DESDEMONA
Alas, what ignorant sin have I committed?   70

OTHELLO
Was this fair paper, this most goodly book,
Made to write "whore" upon? What committed?
Committed? O thou public commoner!   73
I should make very forges of my cheeks   74
That would to cinders burn up modesty,
Did I but speak thy deeds. What committed?
Heaven stops the nose at it, and the moon winks;   77
The bawdy wind, that kisses all it meets,   78
Is hushed within the hollow mine of earth
And will not hear't. What committed?   80
Impudent strumpet!

DESDEMONA   By heaven, you do me wrong!

OTHELLO
Are not you a strumpet?

DESDEMONA   No, as I am a Christian!
If to preserve this vessel for my lord   83
From any other foul unlawful touch
Be not to be a strumpet, I am none.

OTHELLO
What, not a whore?

DESDEMONA   No, as I shall be saved!

---

67 *quicken . . . blowing* i.e., that spring to life as soon as they are deposited;
weed i.e., the wild thing she is, as against, in the next lines, the beautiful
flower she appears to be   70 *committed* (Desdemona's neutral sense of the
word – i.e., "done" – is corrupted by Othello in ll. 72, 73, 76, and 80 to
mean only "commit adultery")   73 *commoner* prostitute, woman used in
common   74–75 *forges . . . modesty* (an image of blushing)   77 *winks* closes
her eyes in shame (the moon symbolizes chastity)   78 *bawdy wind* i.e., indiscriminately lustful, pleasuring everybody   83 *vessel* body

OTHELLO Is't possible?
DESDEMONA
88   O, heaven forgive us!
OTHELLO   I cry you mercy then.
      I took you for that cunning whore of Venice
90   That married with Othello. – *[Calling]* You, mistress,
91   That have the office opposite to Saint Peter
      And keeps the gate of hell!
          Enter Emilia.   You, you, ay, you!
93   We have done our course; there's money for your pains:
      I pray you turn the key, and keep our counsel. *Exit.*
EMILIA
      Alas, what does this gentleman conceive?
      How do you, madam? How do you, my good lady?
97 DESDEMONA Faith, half asleep.
EMILIA
      Good madam, what's the matter with my lord?
DESDEMONA With who?
100 EMILIA Why, with my lord, madam.
DESDEMONA
      Who is thy lord?
EMILIA   He that is yours, sweet lady.
DESDEMONA
      I have none. Do not talk to me, Emilia.
      I cannot weep, nor answers have I none
104   But what should go by water. Prithee tonight
      Lay on my bed my wedding sheets – remember –
      And call thy husband hither.
EMILIA   Here's a change indeed!
                                              Exit.

DESDEMONA
107   'Tis meet I should be used so, very meet.

---

88 *cry you mercy* beg your pardon **91–92** *have . . . hell* (the brothel keeper, the infernal counterpart of Saint Peter, welcomes men to *hell*, another term for the female genitalia) **93** *done our course* finished our business, "had a go" **97** *half asleep* i.e., dazed **104** *go by water* be expressed in tears **107** *meet* proper (referring to Emilia's kindness as opposed to Othello's brutality?)

How have I been behaved, that he might stick
The small'st opinion on my least misuse?   109
   Enter Iago and Emilia.

IAGO
What is your pleasure, madam? How is't with you?   *110*

DESDEMONA
I cannot tell. Those that do teach young babes
Do it with gentle means and easy tasks:
He might have chid me so; for, in good faith,
I am a child to chiding.   114

IAGO   What is the matter, lady?

EMILIA
Alas, Iago, my lord hath so bewhored her,   115
Thrown such despite and heavy terms upon her   116
That true hearts cannot bear it.

DESDEMONA
Am I that name, Iago?

IAGO   What name, fair lady?

DESDEMONA
Such as she said my lord did say I was.

EMILIA
He called her whore. A beggar in his drink   *120*
Could not have laid such terms upon his callet.   121

IAGO
Why did he so?

DESDEMONA
I do not know; I am sure I am none such.

IAGO
Do not weep, do not weep. Alas the day!

EMILIA
Hath she forsook so many noble matches,   125
Her father and her country, and her friends,

---

109 *small'st opinion* worst interpretation (i.e., sexual suspicion); *least misuse*
slightest misconduct 114 *a child to chiding* unused to being scolded 115
bewhored her (1) called her "whore," (2) treated her like a whore 116 *despite*
abuse 121 *callet* slut 125 *forsook* refused; *matches* marriages

To be called whore? Would it not make one weep?

DESDEMONA
It is my wretched fortune.

IAGO   Beshrew him for't!
129   How comes this trick upon him?

DESDEMONA   Nay, heaven doth know.

EMILIA
130   I will be hanged if some eternal villain,
Some busy and insinuating rogue,
132   Some cogging, cozening slave, to get some office,
Have not devised this slander. I will be hanged else.

IAGO
Fie, there is no such man! It is impossible.

DESDEMONA
If any such there be, heaven pardon him!

EMILIA
136   A halter pardon him! and hell gnaw his bones!
Why should he call her whore? Who keeps her company?
What place? what time? what form? what likelihood?
The Moor's abused by some most villainous knave,
140   Some base notorious knave, some scurvy fellow.
141   O heaven, that such companions thou'dst unfold,
And put in every honest hand a whip
· To lash the rascals naked through the world
144   Even from the east to th' west!

IAGO   Speak within door.

EMILIA
145   O, fie upon them! Some such squire he was
146   That turned your wit the seamy side without
And made you to suspect me with the Moor.

---

129 *trick* (1) eccentric behavior, (2) fantasy **130** *eternal* i.e., incorrigible, never-changing **132** *cogging, cozening* cheating, deceiving **136** *halter* noose **140** *scurvy* disgusting, contemptible **141** *companions* rogues, base men (like *fellow* in previous line); *unfold* expose **144** *within door* with greater restraint (i.e., not so loud) **145** *squire* fellow (used contemptuously) **146** *seamy side without* wrong side out

IAGO
   You are a fool. Go to.
DESDEMONA   Alas, Iago,
   What shall I do to win my lord again?
   Good friend, go to him; for, by this light of heaven,   *150*
   I know not how I lost him. Here I kneel:
   If e'er my will did trespass 'gainst his love   152
   Either in discourse of thought or actual deed,   153
   Or that mine eyes, mine ears, or any sense
   Delighted them in any other form,   155
   Or that I do not yet, and ever did,   156
   And ever will (though he do shake me off
   To beggarly divorcement) love him dearly,
   Comfort forswear me! Unkindness may do much,   159
   And his unkindness may defeat my life,   160
   But never taint my love. I cannot say "whore."
   It does abhor me now I speak the word;   162
   To do the act that might the addition earn   163
   Not the world's mass of vanity could make me.   164

IAGO
   I pray you be content. 'Tis but his humor.
   The business of the state does him offense,
   And he does chide with you.
DESDEMONA
   If 'twere no other —
IAGO   It is but so, I warrant.
      [Trumpets within.]
   Hark how these instruments summon to supper.
   The messengers of Venice stays the meat: 170

---

152 *will* desire (with explicit sexual meaning; see note to I.3.321)   153 *discourse of thought* process of thinking   155 *Delighted them* took delight; *form* image, appearance   156 *yet* still, even now   159 *Comfort forswear* let happiness forsake; *Unkindness* unnaturalness (as elsewhere), but also "loss of love"   160 *defeat* destroy   162 *abhor* disgust (with pun on "turn into a whore")   163 *addition* label (i.e., "whore")   164 *vanity* temptations, splendor   170 *stays the meat* await their meal

Go in, and weep not. All things shall be well.
                                    Exeunt Desdemona and Emilia.
        Enter Roderigo.
     How now, Roderigo?
RODERIGO   I do not find that thou deal'st justly with me.
IAGO   What in the contrary?

175   RODERIGO   Every day thou daff'st me with some device,
        Iago, and rather, as it seems to me now, keep'st from me
177   all conveniency than suppliest me with the least advan-
        tage of hope. I will indeed no longer endure it, nor am
        I yet persuaded to put up in peace what already I have
180   foolishly suffered.

IAGO   Will you hear me, Roderigo?

RODERIGO   Faith, I have heard too much; and your
        words and performances are no kin together.

IAGO   You charge me most unjustly.

RODERIGO   With nought but truth. I have wasted myself
        out of my means. The jewels you have had from me to
        deliver Desdemona would half have corrupted a
188   votarist. You have told me she hath received them, and
189   returned me expectations and comforts of sudden re-
190   spect and acquaintance; but I find none.

IAGO   Well, go to; very well.

192   RODERIGO   Very well! go to! I cannot go to, man; nor 'tis
        not very well. Nay, I think it is scurvy, and begin to find
194   myself fopped in it.

IAGO   Very well.

RODERIGO   I tell you 'tis not very well. I will make myself
        known to Desdemona. If she will return me my jewels,
        I will give over my suit and repent my unlawful solici-

---

175 *daff'st . . . device* put me off ("daff" = "doff," remove) with some trick
177 *conveniency* advantage, opportunity   188 *votarist* nun   189–90 *sudden
respect* immediate attention   192 *cannot go to* (Roderigo turns Iago's cliché
[*go to*] into a sexual phrase – i.e., I can't get anywhere with her)   194 *fopped*
made a fool of, duped

tation; if not, assure yourself I will seek satisfaction of   199
you.   200

IAGO   You have said now.

RODERIGO   Ay, and said nothing but what I protest in-
tendment of doing.

IAGO   Why, now I see there's mettle in thee; and even   204
from this instant do build on thee a better opinion than
ever before. Give me thy hand, Roderigo. Thou hast
taken against me a most just exception, but yet I
protest I have dealt most directly in thy affair.   208

RODERIGO   It hath not appeared.

IAGO   I grant indeed it hath not appeared, and your   210
suspicion is not without wit and judgment. But,
Roderigo, if thou hast that in thee indeed which I have
greater reason to believe now than ever – I mean purpose, courage, and valor – this night show it. If thou
the next night following enjoy not Desdemona, take
me from this world with treachery and devise engines   216
for my life.

RODERIGO   Well, what is it? Is it within reason and com-   218
pass?

IAGO   Sir, there is especial commission come from   220
Venice to depute Cassio in Othello's place.

RODERIGO   Is that true? Why, then Othello and Desdemona return again to Venice.

IAGO   O, no; he goes into Mauritania and taketh away   224
with him the fair Desdemona, unless his abode be lin-   225
gered here by some accident; wherein none can be so
determinate as the removing of Cassio.   227

RODERIGO   How do you mean removing him?

---

199 *satisfaction* i.e., "my money back" or equivalent punishment   204 *mettle* spirit, bravery (with pun on "metal," gold)   208 *directly* straightforwardly
216 *engines for* i.e., weapons to take   218–19 *compass* possibility   224
Mauritania a North African realm, home of the Moors   225–26 *abode be lingered here* stay here be extended   227 *determinate* effective

IAGO Why, by making him uncapable of Othello's
230   place – knocking out his brains.
RODERIGO   And that you would have me to do?
IAGO   Ay, if you dare do yourself a profit and a right. He
233   sups tonight with a harlotry, and thither will I go to
       him. He knows not yet of his honorable fortune. If you
       will watch his going thence, which I will fashion to fall
       out between twelve and one, you may take him at your
237   pleasure. I will be near to second your attempt, and he
       shall fall between us. Come, stand not amazed at it, but
       go along with me. I will show you such a necessity in
240   his death that you shall think yourself bound to put it
       on him. It is now high suppertime, and the night grows
       to waste. About it!
RODERIGO   I will hear further reason for this.
IAGO   And you shall be satisfied.   *Exeunt.*

                          *

⌁ **IV.3** *Enter Othello, Lodovico, Desdemona, Emilia,*
      and Attendants.

LODOVICO
   I do beseech you, sir, trouble yourself no further.
OTHELLO
   O, pardon me; 'twill do me good to walk.
LODOVICO
   Madam, good night. I humbly thank your ladyship.
DESDEMONA
   Your honor is most welcome.
OTHELLO   Will you walk, sir?
   O, Desdemona –
DESDEMONA   My lord?

---

233 *harlotry* harlot (i.e., Bianca) 237–38 *he . . . us* i.e., between the two of
us, we can take care of him
   IV.3 A room in the castle

OTHELLO   Get you to bed on th' instant; I will be returned forthwith. Dismiss your attendant there. Look't   8
be done.

DESDEMONA   I will, my lord.   10
            Exit [Othello, with Lodovico and Attendants].

EMILIA   How goes it now? He looks gentler than he did.

DESDEMONA
He says he will return incontinent,   12
And hath commanded me to go to bed,
And bid me to dismiss you.

EMILIA   Dismiss me?

DESDEMONA
It was his bidding; therefore, good Emilia,
Give me my nightly wearing, and adieu.
We must not now displease him.

EMILIA   Ay – would you had never seen him!   18

DESDEMONA
So would not I. My love doth so approve him
That even his stubbornness, his checks, his frowns –   20
Prithee unpin me – have grace and favor.

EMILIA   I have laid those sheets you bade me on the bed.

DESDEMONA
All's one. Good faith, how foolish are our minds!   23
If I do die before thee, prithee shroud me   24
In one of these same sheets.

EMILIA   Come, come! You talk.

DESDEMONA
My mother had a maid called Barbary.   26
She was in love; and he she loved proved mad   27
And did forsake her. She had a song of "Willow";
An old thing 'twas; but it expressed her fortune,
And she died singing it. That song tonight   30

---

8 *forthwith* right away   12 *incontinent* immediately   18 *Ay* – (so Honigmann; most editions read "I would . . .": in the folio "I" can signify both "I"
and "Ay")   20 *stubbornness* roughness; *checks* complaints, rebukes   23 *All's
one* it doesn't matter   24 *shroud me* i.e., wrap my corpse   26 *Barbary* (variant of "Barbara")   27 *mad* wild, unsteady

31   Will not go from my mind; I have much to do
      But to go hang my head all at one side
33   And sing it like poor Barbary. Prithee dispatch.
EMILIA
      Shall I go fetch your nightgown?
DESDEMONA   No, unpin me here.
35   This Lodovico is a proper man.
EMILIA   A very handsome man.
DESDEMONA   He speaks well.
EMILIA   I know a lady in Venice would have walked bare-
      foot to Palestine for a touch of his nether lip.
DESDEMONA   *[Sings.]*
40   "The poor soul sat sighing by a sycamore tree,
41   Sing all a green willow;
      Her hand on her bosom, her head on her knee,
         Sing willow, willow, willow.
      The fresh streams ran by her and murmured her
                     moans;
         Sing willow, willow, willow;
      Her salt tears fell from her, and softened the stones,
         Sing willow, willow, willow."
      Lay by these. – "Willow, willow."
49   Prithee hie thee; he'll come anon.
50   "Sing all a green willow must be my garland.
         Let nobody blame him; his scorn I approve" –
      Nay, that's not next. Hark! who is't that knocks?
EMILIA   It's the wind.
DESDEMONA   *[Sings.]*
      "I called my love false love, but what said he then?
         Sing willow, willow, willow:
      If I court more women, you'll couch with more men."
      So, get thee gone; good night. Mine eyes do itch.

_____

31–32 *I have much to do / But* i.e., it's all I can do not 33 *Prithee dispatch*
please hurry 35 *proper* (1) good-looking, (2) well-behaved 41 *willow*
("weeping" tree identified with unrequited love) 49 *hie thee* hurry

Doth that bode weeping?

EMILIA   'Tis neither here nor there.

DESDEMONA
I have heard it said so. O, these men, these men!
Dost thou in conscience think – tell me, Emilia –   60
That there be women do abuse their husbands   61
In such gross kind?   62

EMILIA   There be some such, no question.

DESDEMONA
Wouldst thou do such a deed for all the world?

EMILIA
Why, would not you?

DESDEMONA   No, by this heavenly light!

EMILIA
Nor I neither by this heavenly light.
I might do't as well i' th' dark.

DESDEMONA
Wouldst thou do such a deed for all the world?

EMILIA The world's a huge thing; it is a great price for a
small vice.

DESDEMONA
In troth, I think thou wouldst not.   70

EMILIA In troth, I think I should; and undo't when I had
done. Marry, I would not do such a thing for a joint   72
ring, nor for measures of lawn, nor for gowns, petti-   73
coats, nor caps, nor any petty exhibition; but, for all the 74
whole world – 'Ud's pity! who would not make her   75
husband a cuckold to make him a monarch? I should
venture purgatory for't.

DESDEMONA
Beshrew me if I would do such a wrong

---

61 *abuse* mistreat (i.e., betray) 62 *In such gross kind* in this wicked way –
i.e., carnally 70 *In troth* by my truth – i.e., faith (a mild oath) 72–73 *joint
ring* ring made in two halves 73 *lawn* linen fabric 74 *exhibition* gift 75
'Ud's God's

    For the whole world.

80 EMILIA   Why, the wrong is but a wrong i' th' world; and
having the world for your labor, 'tis a wrong in your
own world, and you might quickly make it right.

DESDEMONA   I do not think there is any such woman.

84 EMILIA   Yes, a dozen; and as many to th' vantage as
85   would store the world they played for.
    But I do think it is their husbands' faults
    If wives do fall. Say that they slack their duties
88   And pour our treasures into foreign laps;
89   Or else break out in peevish jealousies,
90   Throwing restraint upon us; or say they strike us,
91   Or scant our former having in despite –
92   Why, we have galls, and though we have some grace,
    Yet have we some revenge. Let husbands know
94   Their wives have sense like them. They see, and smell,
    And have their palates both for sweet and sour,
    As husbands have. What is it that they do
    When they change us for others? Is it sport?
98   I think it is. And doth affection breed it?
    I think it doth. Is't frailty that thus errs?
100   It is so too. And have not we affections,
    Desires for sport, and frailty, as men have?
    Then let them use us well; else let them know,
    The ills we do, their ills instruct us so.

DESDEMONA
104   Good night, good night. God me such uses send,
105   Not to pick bad from bad, but by bad mend!   *Exeunt.*

            *

---

84 *dozen* (a hyperbolic understatement); *to th' vantage* in addition   85 *store* populate; *played* gambled (with sexual undertone)   88 *foreign* i.e., strangers' 89 *peevish* unreasonable   90 *Throwing restraint upon us* limiting our freedom, locking us up   91 *scant our former having* reduce our allowance   92 *galls* resentment   94 *sense* sensual feelings   98 *affection* passion, lust   104 *uses* behavior, habits   105 *pick* i.e., pick up, learn

∾ **V.1** *Enter Iago and Roderigo.*

IAGO
> Here, stand behind this bulk; straight will he come.   1
> Wear thy good rapier bare, and put it home.
> Quick, quick! Fear nothing; I'll be at thy elbow.
> It makes us, or it mars us – think on that,
> And fix most firm thy resolution.

RODERIGO
> Be near at hand; I may miscarry in't.

IAGO
> Here, at thy hand. Be bold, and take thy stand.
> *[Stands aside.]*

RODERIGO
> I have no great devotion to the deed,
> And yet he hath given me satisfying reasons.
> 'Tis but a man gone. Forth my sword! He dies!   10

IAGO
> I have rubbed this young quat almost to the sense,   11
> And he grows angry. Now whether he kill Cassio,
> Or Cassio him, or each do kill the other,
> Every way makes my gain. Live Roderigo,   14
> He calls me to a restitution large
> Of gold and jewels that I bobbed from him   16
> As gifts to Desdemona.
> It must not be. If Cassio do remain,
> He hath a daily beauty in his life
> That makes me ugly; and besides, the Moor   20
> May unfold me to him; there stand I in much peril.
> No, he must die. But so! I heard him coming.
> *Enter Cassio.*

V.1 A street in Cyprus 1 *bulk* stall-like structure projecting from a shop
11 *quat* boil, pimple; *sense* quick 14 *Live Roderigo* i.e., if Roderigo lives 16
bobbed swindled

RODERIGO
    I know his gait. 'Tis he. Villain, thou diest!
    [Makes a pass at Cassio.]
CASSIO
    That thrust had been mine enemy indeed
25 But that my coat is better than thou know'st.
    I will make proof of thine.
    [Draws, and wounds Roderigo.]
RODERIGO   O, I am slain!
    *[Iago leaps at Cassio from behind,
    wounds him in the leg, and exits.]*
CASSIO
    I am maimed forever. Help, ho! Murder! murder!
    [Falls.]
    Enter Othello.
OTHELLO
    The voice of Cassio. Iago keeps his word.
RODERIGO
    O, villain that I am!
OTHELLO   It is even so.
CASSIO
30 O, help, ho! light! a surgeon!
OTHELLO
    'Tis he. O brave Iago, honest and just,
    That hast such noble sense of thy friend's wrong!
33 Thou teachest me. Minion, your dear lies dead,
34 And your unblessed fate hies. Strumpet, I come.
35 Forth of my heart those charms, thine eyes, are blotted.
    Thy bed, lust-stained, shall with lust's blood be spot-
        ted.   *Exit Othello.*
    Enter Lodovico and Gratiano.
CASSIO
37 What, ho? No watch? No passage? Murder! murder!

---

25 *coat* i.e., soldier's undercoat of mail   33 *Minion* darling, favorite (here ad-
dressed contemptuously to Desdemona)   34 *hies* comes quickly   35 *Forth
of* i.e., out of   37 *watch* night watchmen; *passage* traffic, passersby

GRATIANO
   'Tis some mischance. The voice is very direful.
CASSIO   O, help!
LODOVICO   Hark! ·   40
RODERIGO   O wretched villain!
LODOVICO
   Two or three groan. 'Tis heavy night.   42
   These may be counterfeits. Let's think't unsafe
   To come into the cry without more help.
RODERIGO
   Nobody come? Then shall I bleed to death.
LODOVICO   Hark!
     Enter Iago [with a light].
GRATIANO
   Here's one comes in his shirt, with light and weapons.   47
IAGO
   Who's there? Whose noise is this that cries on murder?   48
LODOVICO
   We do not know.
IAGO   Do not you hear a cry?
CASSIO
   Here, here! For heaven sake, help me!   50
IAGO   What's the matter?
GRATIANO
   This is Othello's ancient, as I take it.
LODOVICO
   The same indeed, a very valiant fellow.
IAGO
   What are you here that cry so grievously?
CASSIO
   Iago? O, I am spoiled, undone by villains!   54
   Give me some help.
IAGO
   O me, lieutenant! What villains have done this?

---

42 *heavy* dismal, dark   47 *shirt* i.e., without his jacket, not fully dressed **48**
on of   54 *spoiled* ruined (i.e., injured)

CASSIO
   I think that one of them is hereabout
58 And cannot make away.
IAGO   O treacherous villains!
   [To Lodovico and Gratiano]
   What are you there? Come in, and give some help.
RODERIGO
60 O, help me there!
CASSIO
   That's one of them.
IAGO   O murd'rous slave! O villain!
   [Stabs Roderigo.]
RODERIGO
   O damned Iago! O inhuman dog!
IAGO
   Kill men i' th' dark? – Where be these bloody thieves? –
   How silent is this town! – Ho! murder! murder! –
   What may you be? Are you of good or evil?
LODOVICO
66 As you shall prove us, praise us.
IAGO   Signor Lodovico?
LODOVICO   He, sir.
IAGO
   I cry you mercy. Here's Cassio hurt by villains.
70 GRATIANO   Cassio?
IAGO   How is't, brother?
CASSIO
   My leg is cut in two.
IAGO   Marry, heaven forbid!
   Light, gentlemen. I'll bind it with my shirt.
   Enter Bianca.
BIANCA
   What is the matter, ho? Who is't that cried?

---

58 *make away* escape 66 *prove us, praise us* i.e., put us to the test and you'll
see (*praise*=appraise)

IAGO
  Who is't that cried?
BIANCA
  O my dear Cassio! my sweet Cassio!
  O Cassio, Cassio, Cassio!
IAGO
  O notable strumpet! – Cassio, may you suspect
  Who they should be that have thus mangled you?
CASSIO   No.   80
GRATIANO   I am sorry to find you thus. I have been to
  seek you.
IAGO
  Lend me a garter. So. – O for a chair   83
  To bear him easily hence!
BIANCA
  Alas, he faints! O Cassio, Cassio, Cassio!
IAGO
  Gentlemen all, I do suspect this trash   86
  To be a party in this injury. –
  Patience awhile, good Cassio. – Come, come!
  Lend me a light. Know we this face or no?
  Alas, my friend and my dear countryman   90
  Roderigo? No. – Yes, sure. – O heaven, Roderigo!
GRATIANO   What, of Venice?
IAGO
  Even he, sir. Did you know him?
GRATIANO   Know him? Ay.
IAGO
  Signor Gratiano? I cry your gentle pardon.   94
  These bloody accidents must excuse my manners   95
  That so neglected you.
GRATIANO   I am glad to see you.
IAGO
  How do you, Cassio? – O, a chair, a chair!

---

83 *garter* i.e., for a tourniquet; *chair* litter (a framework couch for carrying
the wounded) 86 *trash* i.e., Bianca 94 *cry* beg 95 *accidents* sudden events

GRATIANO   Roderigo?

IAGO

99   He, he, 'tis he!

    [A litter brought in.]

                O, that's well said; the chair.

100   Some good man bear him carefully from hence.

    I'll fetch the general's surgeon.

    [To Bianca]   For you, mistress,

102   Save you your labor. – He that lies slain here, Cassio,

    Was my dear friend. What malice was between you?

CASSIO

    None in the world, nor do I know the man.

IAGO   *[To Bianca]*

    What, look you pale? – O, bear him out o' th' air.

            [Cassio and Roderigo are borne off.]

    Stay you, good gentlemen. – Look you pale, mistress? –

107   Do you perceive the gastness of her eye? –

    Nay, if you stare, we shall hear more anon.

    Behold her well; I pray you look upon her.

110   Do you see, gentlemen? Nay, guiltiness will speak,

    Though tongues were out of use.

    [Enter Emilia.]

EMILIA

    Alas, what is the matter? What is the matter, husband?

IAGO

    Cassio hath here been set on in the dark

    By Roderigo, and fellows that are scaped.

    He's almost slain, and Roderigo quite dead.

EMILIA

    Alas, good gentleman! alas, good Cassio!

IAGO

    This is the fruits of whoring. Prithee, Emilia,

    Go know of Cassio where he supped tonight.

    [To Bianca]

---

99 *well said* i.e., well done   **102** *Save . . . labor* i.e., you needn't fuss about him anymore; leave him alone   **107** *gastness* ghastly look, fear

What, do you shake at that?

BIANCA

He supped at my house; but I therefore shake not.   120

IAGO

O did he so? I charge you go with me.

EMILIA

O, fie upon thee, strumpet!   122

BIANCA

I am no strumpet, but of life as honest   123
As you that thus abuse me.

EMILIA   As I? Fie upon thee!

IAGO

Kind gentlemen, let's go see poor Cassio dressed.   125
     [To Bianca]
Come, mistress, you must tell's another tale.
Emilia, run you to the citadel
And tell my lord and lady what hath happed.
                                        [Exit Emilia.]
Will you go on afore?   *Exeunt [all but Iago].*
                    This is the night
That either makes me or fordoes me quite.   *[Exit.]* 130

                              *

❧ **V.2** *Enter Othello [with a light], and Desdemona
[asleep] in her bed.*

OTHELLO

It is the cause, it is the cause, my soul.   1
Let me not name it to you, you chaste stars!
It is the cause. Yet I'll not shed her blood,
Nor scar that whiter skin of hers than snow,

---

122 *fie* i.e., shame   123 *honest* chaste   125 *dressed* bandaged   130 *fordoes*
destroys, undoes
     V.2 A bedroom in the castle   1 *cause* (1) legal matter or "case" (here, the
crime of adultery), (2) principle (i.e., not merely a personal grievance); *my
soul* (conventional form of self-address)

5   And smooth as monumental alablaster.
       Yet she must die, else she'll betray more men.
       Put out the light, and then put out the light.
8   If I quench thee, thou flaming minister,
       I can again thy former light restore,
10   Should I repent me; but once put out thy light,
11   Thou cunning'st pattern of excelling nature,
12   I know not where is that Promethean heat
13   That can thy light relume. When I have plucked thy
          rose,
       I cannot give it vital growth again;
       It needs must wither. I'll smell thee on the tree.
          [He kisses her.]
       O balmy breath, that dost almost persuade
       Justice to break her sword! One more, one more!
       Be thus when thou art dead, and I will kill thee,
       And love thee after. One more, and that's the last!
20   So sweet was ne'er so fatal. I must weep,
21   But they are cruel tears. This sorrow's heavenly;
       It strikes where it doth love. She wakes.
       DESDEMONA
       Who's there? Othello?
       OTHELLO   Ay, Desdemona.
       DESDEMONA
       Will you come to bed, my lord?
       OTHELLO
       Have you prayed tonight, Desdemon?
       DESDEMONA   Ay, my lord.
       OTHELLO
26   If you bethink yourself of any crime

---

5 *alablaster* alabaster, white marble (the archaic form retained here for its
sound) 8 *flaming minister* i.e., the torch or candle that, as *minister* or servant, lights the chamber 11 *Thou . . . nature* i.e., Desdemona (*cunning'st*=beautifully made) 12 *Promethean heat* divine spark (Prometheus
legendarily stole fire from heaven) 13 *relume* rekindle 21 *cruel* i.e., un-
merciful, but perhaps "painful" or "distressing" 21–22 *sorrow's . . . love* (see
Hebrews 12:6, "whom the Lord loveth he chasteneth") 26 *crime* sin

Unreconciled as yet to heaven and grace,
Solicit for it straight.   28

DESDEMONA
Alack, my lord, what may you mean by that?

OTHELLO
Well, do it, and be brief; I will walk by.   30
I would not kill thy unpreparèd spirit.
No, heavens forfend! I would not kill thy soul.   32

DESDEMONA
Talk you of killing?

OTHELLO   Ay, I do.

DESDEMONA   Then heaven
Have mercy on me!

OTHELLO   Amen, with all my heart!

DESDEMONA
If you say so, I hope you will not kill me.

OTHELLO   Humh.

DESDEMONA
And yet I fear you; for you're fatal then   37
When your eyes roll so. Why I should fear I know not,
Since guiltiness I know not; but yet I feel I fear.

OTHELLO
Think on thy sins.   40

DESDEMONA   They are loves I bear to you.

OTHELLO
Ay, and for that thou diest.

DESDEMONA
That death's unnatural that kills for loving.
Alas, why gnaw you so your nether lip?
Some bloody passion shakes your very frame.
These are portents; but yet I hope, I hope,   45
They do not point on me.   46

OTHELLO   Peace and be still!

---

28 *Solicit* i.e., pray for forgiveness **32** *forfend* forbid **37** *fatal* ominous,
frightening **40** *They . . . you* i.e., my only sin is in loving you too much
(more than God) **45** *portents* omens, usually bad **46** *still* quiet

DESDEMONA
I will so. What's the matter?
OTHELLO
That handkerchief which I so loved and gave thee
Thou gav'st to Cassio.
DESDEMONA   No, by my life and soul!
50   Send for the man and ask him.
OTHELLO   Sweet soul, take heed,
51   Take heed of perjury; thou art on thy deathbed.
DESDEMONA
52   Ay, but not yet to die.
OTHELLO   Presently.
Therefore confess thee freely of thy sin,
For to deny each article with oath
55   Cannot remove nor choke the strong conception
56   That I do groan withal. Thou art to die.
DESDEMONA
Then Lord have mercy on me!
OTHELLO   I say amen.
DESDEMONA
And have you mercy too! I never did
59   Offend you in my life; never loved Cassio
60   But with such general warranty of heaven
As I might love. I never gave him token.
OTHELLO
By heaven, I saw my handkerchief in's hand!
63   O perjured woman! thou dost stone my heart,
And makes me call what I intend to do
A murder, which I thought a sacrifice.
I saw the handkerchief.
DESDEMONA   He found it then.
I never gave it him. Send for him hither.

---

51 *deathbed* (i.e., women were sometimes buried in their wedding sheets)
52 *Presently* right away 55 *conception* belief, or perhaps "plan," "intention,"
preparing for the metaphor in the next line of aborted childbirth 56 *groan
withal* i.e., labor to give birth to (but with the modern sense of "moan in sorrow") 59 *Offend* wrong 63 *stone my heart* i.e., turn it to stone

Let him confess a truth.
OTHELLO   He hath confessed.
DESDEMONA
What, my lord?
OTHELLO
That he hath used thee.   70
DESDEMONA   How? unlawfully?
OTHELLO   Ay.
DESDEMONA
He will not say so.
OTHELLO   No, his mouth is stopped.
Honest Iago hath ta'en order for't.   72
DESDEMONA
O, my fear interprets. What, is he dead?   73
OTHELLO
Had all his hairs been lives, my great revenge
Had stomach for them all.   75
DESDEMONA
Alas, he is betrayed, and I undone!
OTHELLO
Out, strumpet! Weep'st thou for him to my face?
DESDEMONA
O, banish me, my lord, but kill me not!
OTHELLO
Down, strumpet!
DESDEMONA
Kill me tomorrow; let me live tonight!   80
OTHELLO
Nay, if you strive —   81
DESDEMONA
But half an hour!   82
OTHELLO   Being done, there is no pause.
DESDEMONA
But while I say one prayer!

---

72 *ta'en order* arranged   73 *interprets* guesses (the worst)   75 *stomach* appetite, desire   81 *strive* struggle   82 *Being done* i.e., since the case is over

OTHELLO   It is too late.
    Smothers her.
DESDEMONA   O Lord, Lord, Lord!
    Emilia at the door.
EMILIA   *[Calls within.]*
    My lord, my lord! What, ho! my lord, my lord!
OTHELLO
    What noise is this? Not dead? not yet quite dead?
    I that am cruel am yet merciful;
    I would not have thee linger in thy pain.
    So, so.
EMILIA   *Within*
90 What, ho! my lord, my lord!
OTHELLO   Who's there?
EMILIA   *[Within]*
    O, good my lord, I would speak a word with you!
OTHELLO
92 Yes, 'tis Emilia. – By and by. – She's dead. –
    'Tis like she comes to speak of Cassio's death.
94 The noise was high. Ha! no more moving?
    Still as the grave. – Shall she come in? Were't good? –
    I think she stirs again. No. – What's best to do?
    If she come in, she'll sure speak to my wife.
    My wife! my wife! what wife? I have no wife.
    O, insupportable! O heavy hour!
100 Methinks it should be now a huge eclipse
    Of sun and moon, and that th' affrighted globe
102 Did yawn at alteration.
EMILIA   *[Within]*   I do beseech you
    That I may speak with you, O good my lord!
OTHELLO
    I had forgot thee. O, come in, Emilia.
    Soft, by and by. – Let me the curtains draw. –
    [Closes the bed curtains.]

---

92 *By and by* coming, just a moment (to Emilia)   94 *high* loud   102 *yawn
at alteration* split open (in an earthquake) at the change brought on by Desdemona's death

Where art thou?
[Opens the door.]
Enter Emilia.
                What's the matter with thee now?

EMILIA
O my good lord, yonder's foul murders done!

OTHELLO   What? Now?

EMILIA   But now, my lord.   109

OTHELLO
It is the very error of the moon.   110
She comes more nearer earth than she was wont   111
And makes men mad.

EMILIA
Cassio, my lord, hath killed a young Venetian
Called Roderigo.

OTHELLO   Roderigo killed?
And Cassio killed?

EMILIA   No, Cassio is not killed.

OTHELLO
Not Cassio killed? Then murder's out of tune,
And sweet revenge grows harsh.

DESDEMONA
O, falsely, falsely murdered!

EMILIA   O Lord! what cry is that?

OTHELLO   That? What?

EMILIA
Out and alas! that was my lady's voice.   *120*
Help! help, ho! help! O lady, speak again!
Sweet Desdemona! O sweet mistress, speak!

DESDEMONA
A guiltless death I die.

EMILIA
O, who hath done this deed?

---

109 *But* just   110 *error* wandering, errancy, with dire earthly consequences
111 *was wont* was formerly accustomed to do

DESDEMONA

Nobody – I myself. Farewell.

126 Commend me to my kind lord. O, farewell!

[She dies.]

OTHELLO

Why, how should she be murdered?

EMILIA   Alas, who knows?

OTHELLO

You heard her say herself, it was not I.

EMILIA

She said so. I must needs report the truth.

OTHELLO

130 She's like a liar gone to burning hell!

'Twas I that killed her.

EMILIA   O, the more angel she,

And you the blacker devil!

OTHELLO

She turned to folly, and she was a whore.

EMILIA

Thou dost belie her, and thou art a devil.

OTHELLO

135 She was false as water.

EMILIA   Thou art rash as fire to say

That she was false. O, she was heavenly true!

OTHELLO

137 Cassio did top her. Ask thy husband else.

O, I were damned beneath all depth in hell

139 But that I did proceed upon just grounds

140 To this extremity. Thy husband knew it all.

EMILIA   My husband?

OTHELLO   Thy husband.

EMILIA

That she was false to wedlock?

---

126 *Commend* remember, speak of 135 *water* (considered unstable or changing) 137 *top* (see *tupping*, I.1.88); *else* i.e., if you want to know more (*else*) 139 *But that . . . grounds* i.e., if I had acted without justification

OTHELLO
Ay, with Cassio. Had she been true,
If heaven would make me such another world   145
Of one entire and perfect chrysolite,   146
I'd not have sold her for it.

EMILIA
My husband?

OTHELLO   Ay, 'twas he that told me on her first.
An honest man he is, and hates the slime
That sticks on filthy deeds.   150

EMILIA   My husband?

OTHELLO
What needs this iterance, woman? I say thy husband.   151

EMILIA
O mistress, villainy hath made mocks with love!   152
My husband say she was false?

OTHELLO   He, woman.
I say, thy husband. Dost understand the word?
My friend, thy husband; honest, honest Iago.

EMILIA
If he say so, may his pernicious soul
Rot half a grain a day! he lies to th' heart.   157
She was too fond of her most filthy bargain.   158

OTHELLO   Ha!

EMILIA   Do thy worst.   160
This deed of thine is no more worthy heaven
Than thou wast worthy her.

OTHELLO   Peace, you were best.

EMILIA
Thou hast not half that power to do me harm
As I have to be hurt. O gull! O dolt!   164
As ignorant as dirt! thou has done a deed –

---

145 *such another world* i.e., another world like this one   146 *chrysolite* precious gem   151 *iterance* repetition   152 *made mocks with* played games with   157 *half a grain a day* i.e., slowly and painfully   158 *fond . . . bargain* i.e., devoted to her vows to you   164 *to be hurt* to endure pain; *gull* (common word for a dupe, someone easy to cheat)

I care not for thy sword; I'll make thee known,
Though I lost twenty lives. Help! help! ho! help!
The Moor hath killed my mistress! Murder! murder!
Enter Montano, Gratiano, and Iago [with others].

MONTANO
What is the matter? How now, general?

EMILIA

170   O, are you come, Iago? You have done well,
171   That men must lay their murders on your neck.

GRATIANO
What is the matter?

EMILIA
Disprove this villain, if thou be'st a man.
He says thou told'st him that his wife was false.
I know thou didst not; thou'rt not such a villain.
Speak, for my heart is full.

IAGO
I told him what I thought, and told no more
Than what he found himself was apt and true.

EMILIA
But did you ever tell him she was false?

180   IAGO   I did.

EMILIA
You told a lie, an odious damnèd lie!
Upon my soul, a lie! a wicked lie!
She false with Cassio? Did you say with Cassio?

IAGO

184   With Cassio, mistress. Go to, charm your tongue.

EMILIA
I will not charm my tongue; I am bound to speak:
My mistress here lies murdered in her bed –

ALL
O heavens forfend!

---

171 *lay . . . neck* charge you with murder   **184** *charm* cast a spell on (i.e., silence)

EMILIA

And your reports have set the murder on.

OTHELLO

Nay, stare not, masters. It is true indeed.

GRATIANO

'Tis a strange truth.   *190*

MONTANO

O monstrous act!

EMILIA   Villainy, villainy, villainy!

I think upon't – I think I smell't! – O villainy!

I thought so then. – I'll kill myself for grief. –

O villainy, villainy!

IAGO

What, are you mad? I charge you get you home.

EMILIA

Good gentlemen, let me have leave to speak.

'Tis proper I obey him, but not now.

Perchance, Iago, I will ne'er go home.

OTHELLO

O! O! O!

[Falls on the bed.]

EMILIA   Nay, lay thee down and roar!

For thou hast killed the sweetest innocent   *200*

That e'er did lift up eye.   *201*

OTHELLO   O, she was foul!

[Rises.]

I scarce did know you, uncle. There lies your niece,

Whose breath, indeed, these hands have newly stopped.

I know this act shows horrible and grim.   *204*

GRATIANO

Poor Desdemon! I am glad thy father's dead.

Thy match was mortal to him, and pure grief

Shore his old thread in twain. Did he live now,   *207*

This sight would make him do a desperate turn,   *208*

---

201 *lift up eye* i.e., to heaven in prayer **204** *shows* appears **207** *Shore* cut
208 *turn* act

Yea, curse his better angel from his side,
210   And fall to reprobance.

OTHELLO
'Tis pitiful; but yet Iago knows
That she with Cassio hath the act of shame
A thousand times committed. Cassio confessed it,
214   And she did gratify his amorous works
215   With that recognizance and pledge of love
Which I first gave her. I saw it in his hand.
It was a handkerchief, an antique token
My father gave my mother.

EMILIA
O God! O heavenly God!

IAGO
220   Zounds, hold your peace!

EMILIA   'Twill out, 'twill out! I peace?
221   No, I will speak as liberal as the north.
Let heaven and men and devils, let them all,
All, all, cry shame against me, yet I'll speak.

IAGO
Be wise, and get you home.

EMILIA   I will not.
       [Iago draws and threatens Emilia.]

GRATIANO   Fie!
Your sword upon a woman?

EMILIA
O thou dull Moor, that handkerchief thou speak'st of
I found by fortune, and did give my husband;
For often with a solemn earnestness –
More than indeed belonged to such a trifle –
230   He begged of me to steal't.

IAGO   Villainous whore!

---

210 *reprobance* the state of rejection by God   **214** *gratify . . . works* reward
his sexual acts   **215** *recognizance* token   **221** *as liberal as the north* as freely
as the north wind blows

EMILIA
  She give it Cassio? No, alas, I found it,
  And I did give't my husband.
IAGO   Filth, thou liest!
EMILIA
  By heaven, I do not, I do not, gentlemen.
  O murd'rous coxcomb! what should such a fool   234
  Do with so good a wife?   235
OTHELLO   Are there no stones in heaven
  But what serves for the thunder? Precious villain!   236
    [The Moor runs at Iago but is disarmed.
    Iago stabs his wife.]
GRATIANO
  The woman falls. Sure he hath killed his wife.
EMILIA
  Ay, ay. O, lay me by my mistress' side.   *[Exit Iago.]*
GRATIANO
  He's gone, but his wife's killed.
MONTANO
  'Tis a notorious villain. Take you this weapon,   240
  Which I have here recovered from the Moor.
  Come, guard the door without. Let him not pass,
  But kill him rather. I'll after that same villain,
  For 'tis a damnèd slave.
    Exit [Montano, with all but Othello and Emilia].
OTHELLO   I am not valiant neither;
  But every puny whipster gets my sword.   245
  But why should honor outlive honesty?   246
  Let it go all.
EMILIA   What did thy song bode, lady?

---

234 *coxcomb* jester, fool (i.e., Othello)   235–36 *Are there . . . the thunder*
i.e., why doesn't heaven rain down stones on this villain   236 *Precious* utter
240 *a notorious* an extraordinary, incredible (i.e., not the modern "well-
known")   245 *puny whipster* foolish, insignificant person (cf. whippersnap-
per)   246 *honor* i.e., military achievement; *honesty* chastity

248 Hark, canst thou hear me? I will play the swan,
     And die in music. *[Sings.]* "Willow, willow, willow."
250 Moor, she was chaste. She loved thee, cruel Moor:
     So come my soul to bliss as I speak true.
     So speaking as I think, alas, I die.
       [She dies.]
OTHELLO
     I have another weapon in this chamber;
254 It was a sword of Spain, the ice brook's temper.
     O, here it is. – Uncle, I must come forth.
GRATIANO   *[Within]*
     If thou attempt it, it will cost thee dear.
     Thou hast no weapon, and perforce must suffer.
OTHELLO
     Look in upon me then and speak with me,
259 Or, naked as I am, I will assault thee.
       [Enter Gratiano.]
GRATIANO
260 What is the matter?
OTHELLO   Behold, I have a weapon;
     A better never did itself sustain
     Upon a soldier's thigh. I have seen the day
     That with this little arm and this good sword
     I have made my way through more impediments
265 Than twenty times your stop. But O vain boast!
     Who can control his fate? 'Tis not so now.
     Be not afraid, though you do see me weaponed.
268 Here is my journey's end, here is my butt
269 And very seamark of my utmost sail:
270 Do you go back dismayed? 'Tis a lost fear.
271 Man but a rush against Othello's breast

248–49 *swan . . . music* (according to legend, the ordinarily mute swan sang beautifully just before death) **254** *sword . . . temper* i.e., Spanish sword hardened or tempered in freezing water **259** *naked* unarmed **265** *your stop* i.e., the obstacle you impose **268** *butt* target (from archery) **269** *seamark . . . sail* beacon or destination of my last voyage **270** *lost* wasted **271** *Man but a rush* i.e., use only a reed

And he retires. Where should Othello go?   272
Now, how dost thou look now? O ill-starred wench!
Pale as thy smock! When we shall meet at compt,   274
This look of thine will hurl my soul from heaven,
And fiends will snatch at it. Cold, cold, my girl?
Even like thy chastity.
O cursèd, cursèd slave! Whip me, ye devils,
From the possession of this heavenly sight!
Blow me about in winds! roast me in sulphur!   280
Wash me in steep-down gulfs of liquid fire!
Oh Desdemon! dead Desdemon! dead! Oh! Oh!
    *Enter Lodovico, Cassio [in a litter], Montano, and
    Iago, with Officers.*

LODOVICO
Where is this rash and most unfortunate man?

OTHELLO
That's he that was Othello. Here I am.

LODOVICO
Where is that viper? Bring the villain forth.

OTHELLO
I look down towards his feet – but that's a fable.   286
If that thou be'st a devil, I cannot kill thee.
    [Wounds Iago.]

LODOVICO
Wrench his sword from him.
    [Othello is disarmed.]

IAGO   I bleed, sir, but not killed.

OTHELLO
I am not sorry neither. I'd have thee live,
For in my sense, 'tis happiness to die.   290

LODOVICO
O thou Othello that was once so good,
Fall'n in the practice of a damnèd slave,   292

---

272 *retires* withdraws, retreats (a military term)   274 *compt* i.e., final ac-
counting (Last Judgment)   286 *I . . . fable* (Othello inspects Iago's feet to
test the legend that the devil's feet are cloven)   292 *practice* plot

What shall be said to thee?

OTHELLO   Why, anything:
An honorable murderer, if you will;
For nought I did in hate, but all in honor.

LODOVICO
This wretch hath part confessed his villainy.

297   Did you and he consent in Cassio's death?

OTHELLO   Ay.

CASSIO
Dear general, I never gave you cause.

OTHELLO

300   I do believe it, and I ask your pardon.

301   Will you, I pray, demand that demidevil
Why he hath thus ensnared my soul and body?

IAGO
Demand me nothing. What you know, you know.
From this time forth I never will speak word.

LODOVICO
What, not to pray?

GRATIANO   Torments will ope your lips.

OTHELLO
Well, thou dost best.

LODOVICO
Sir, you shall understand what hath befall'n,
Which, as I think, you know not. Here is a letter
Found in the pocket of the slain Roderigo,

310   And here another. The one of them imports
The death of Cassio to be undertook
By Roderigo.

OTHELLO

313   O villain!

CASSIO   Most heathenish and most gross!

LODOVICO
Now here's another discontented paper

---

297 *consent in* agree (in planning)   **301** *demidevil* half demon, almost a devil
313 *gross* monstrous

Found in his pocket too, and this, it seems,
Roderigo meant t' have sent this damnèd villain;
But that, belike, Iago in the interim
Came in and satisfied him.   318

OTHELLO   O thou pernicious caitiff! –
How came you, Cassio, by that handkerchief
That was my wife's?   320

CASSIO   I found it in my chamber;
And he himself confessed it but even now
That there he dropped it for a special purpose
Which wrought to his desire.

OTHELLO   O fool! fool! fool!

CASSIO
There is besides in Roderigo's letter,
How he upbraids Iago that he made him
Brave me upon the watch, whereon it came   326
That I was cast; and even but now he spake,   327
After long seeming dead – Iago hurt him,
Iago set him on.

LODOVICO
You must forsake this room and go with us.   330
Your power and your command is taken off,
And Cassio rules in Cyprus. For this slave,
If there be any cunning cruelty
That can torment him much and hold him long,   334
It shall be his. You shall close prisoner rest   335
Till that the nature of your fault be known
To the Venetian state. Come, bring away.

OTHELLO
Soft you! a word or two before you go.   338
I have done the state some service, and they know't.
No more of that. I pray you, in your letters,   340

---

318 *caitiff* villain   326 *Brave* defy, challenge   327 *cast* dismissed   334 *hold
him long* i.e., keep him alive through torture   335 *close prisoner rest* i.e., remain closely guarded, confined   338 *Soft you* one moment, wait

341   When you shall these unlucky deeds relate,
342   Speak of me as I am. Nothing extenuate,
       Nor set down aught in malice. Then must you speak
       Of one that loved not wisely, but too well;
345   Of one not easily jealous, but, being wrought,
346   Perplexed in the extreme; of one whose hand,
347   Like the base Judean, threw a pearl away
348   Richer than all his tribe; of one whose subdued eyes,
       Albeit unusèd to the melting mood,
350   Drops tears as fast as the Arabian trees
351   Their medicinable gum. Set you down this.
       And say besides that in Aleppo once,
       Where a malignant and a turbaned Turk
354   Beat a Venetian and traduced the state,
       I took by th' throat the circumcisèd dog
       And smote him – thus.
            [He stabs himself.]

LODOVICO
357   O bloody period!

GRATIANO   All that is spoke is marred.

OTHELLO
       I kissed thee ere I killed thee. No way but this,
       Killing myself, to die upon a kiss.
            [He] dies.

CASSIO
360   This did I fear, but thought he had no weapon;
361   For he was great of heart.

LODOVICO   *[To Iago]*   O Spartan dog,
362   More fell than anguish, hunger, or the sea!
       Look on the tragic loading of this bed.

----

341 *unlucky* unfortunate 342 *extenuate* soft-pedal (literally, "thin out")
345 *wrought* worked up, worked on 346 *Perplexed* desperate, bewildered
347 *base Judean* (perhaps Judas Iscariot, betrayer of Christ, or Herod, who
impulsively killed his wife; Q reads "Indian") 348 *subdued* conquered,
overcome with grief 351 *gum* i.e., myrrh 354 *traduced* betrayed 357 *period* ending 361 *Spartan dog* (bloodhound known for silence) 362 *fell*
merciless, inhuman

This is thy work. The object poisons sight;
Let it be hid. Gratiano, keep the house,   365
And seize upon the fortunes of the Moor,   366
For they succeed on you. To you, lord governor,   367
Remains the censure of this hellish villain,   368
The time, the place, the torture. O, enforce it!
Myself will straight aboard, and to the state   370
This heavy act with heavy heart relate.   *Exeunt.*

---

365 *Let it be hid* i.e., draw the bed curtains; *keep* guard   366 *seize upon* take
legal control of   367 *succeed on* pass to you (as Desdemona's uncle) by in-
heritance   368 *censure* judgment, passing sentence

AVAILABLE FROM PENGUIN CLASSICS

The legendary Pelican Shakespeare series features authoritative and meticulously researched texts paired with scholarship by renowned Shakespeareans. Updated for the twenty-first century by general editors Stephen Orgel and A. R. Braunmuller, each book includes an essay on the theatrical world of Shakespeare's time, an introduction to the individual play, and a detailed note on the text used. These easy-to-read editions incorporate over thirty years of Shakespeare scholarship undertaken since the original series, edited by Alfred Harbage, appeared between 1956 and 1967. Offering dependable texts and illuminating essays, the Pelican Shakespeare will remain a valued resource for students, teachers, and theater professionals for many years to come.

All's Well That Ends Well

Antony and Cleopatra

As You Like It

The Comedy of Errors

*The Complete Pelican
Shakespeare*

Coriolanus

Cymbeline

Hamlet

Henry IV, Part I

Henry IV, Part 2

Henry V

Henry VI, Part I

Henry VI, Part 2

Henry VI, Part 3

Henry VIII

Julius Caesar

King John

King Lear

*King Lear
(The Quarto and Folio Texts)*

Love's Labor's Lost

Macbeth

PENGUIN CLASSICS

AVAILABLE FROM PENGUIN CLASSICS

PENGUIN CLASSICS

The Complete Pelican Shakespeare

Since the Pelican Shakespeare Series debuted more than fifty years ago, developments in scholarship have revolutionized our understanding of William Shakespeare. The general editors of the series, world-renowned Shakespeareans Stephen Orgel and A.R. Braunmuller, dedicated seven years to incorporating the most up-to-date research and debate about the Bard, making this revised edition of the complete works the premier choice for students, teachers, academics, and general readers for decades to come.

PENGUIN CLASSICS